Movers and Shakers

Prominent Ottumwa Businessmen 1913-1914

Leigh Michaels

PBL Limited
Ottumwa Iowa

Copyright 2018 by Leigh Michaels

Cover and design copyright 2018 by Leigh Michaels

This edition published 2018

10 9 8 7 6 5 4 3 2 1

ISBN 1-892689-77-4
ISBN 13: 978-1-892689-77-1

Printed in the United States of America

Illustrations: Caricatures originally published by The Ottumwa *Courier*. Additional images are from History of Wapello County (Waterman, 1914) and other Wapello County histories; from scrapbooks collected by the Ottumwa Public Library, from the Ottumwa *Courier,* and courtesy of The Lemberger Collection. Ads are from the McCoy City Directory of 1913-14 or from the Ottumwa *Courier* (microfilm courtesy of Ottumwa Public Library).

All rights reserved. Except for brief passages quoted in any review, the reproduction or utilization of this work in whole or in part, in any form or by any electronic, mechanical, or other means, now known or hereinafter invented, including xerography, photocopying and recording, or in any information storage and retrieval system, is forbidden without the express permission of the publisher. For permission contact:
    Rights Editor
    PBL Limited
    P.O. Box 935
    Ottumwa IA 52501-0935
    www.pbllimited.com

Visit our website at www.pbllimited.com for more information about this and other publications. Quantity and wholesale prices are available.

Cover illustration: Fifth Street, looking east from Washington Street toward North Court Street, about 1910. First Baptist Church is at center. The tower of Trinity Episcopal Church is visible on the horizon at center left, and the houses at right center remain in use.

> For Kevin
> who inspires me
> to be a better person

Christmas ads, December 1913 Courier

Why would it not be a good idea to remember

Mother

Wife or

Sister

with one of the beautiful Cabinet Gas Ranges, used a thousand times a year or a Gas Iron neatly packed in holly boxes. Delivered anytime, connected free

Gas Cake Griddles

Gas Portable Lamps

Gas Waffle Irons or Toasters

Gas Company

Contents

Introduction 6

The Businessmen 8

(Names are listed here as they appeared in the original newspaper publication)

L.A. Andrew 8
W.T. Archer 10
John T. Bohe 12
J.D. Browning 14
L.R. Clausen 16
Seneca Cornell 18
William Cramblit 20
F.B. Cresswell 22
L.T. Crisman 24
F.L. Daggett 26
W.R. Daggett 28
J.B. Dennis 30
J.F. Dings 32
W.J. Donelan 34
J.K. Dysart 36
Dr. E.T. Edgerly 38
H.L. Edmunds 40
E.E. England 42
C.E. Fahrney 44
Julius Fecht 46
Wm. Fiedler 48
T.D. Foster 50
E.D. Fowler 52
N. Friedman 54
J.W. Garner 56
T.E. Gibbons 58
J.T. Hackworth 60
Chas. Hallberg 62
C.S. Harper 64
W.T. Harper 66
A.G. Harrow 68

Carl T. Haw 70
B. Hofmann 72
Frank P. Hofmann 74
Judge F.M. Hunter 76
M.B. Hutchison 78
W.H.C. Jacques 80
Allen Johnston 82
W.E. Jones 84
W.H. Keating 86
Thos. F. Keefe 88
G.M. Kerns 90
L.M. Kidd 92
Dr W.B. LaForce 94
E.L. Lambert 96
A. Lowenberg 98
H.J. Lytle 100
J.M. Majors 102
Calvin Manning 104
J.B. McCarroll 106
C.W. McCarty 108
C.E. McDaniel 110
Ralph T. McElroy 112
Walter H. McElroy 114
Frank McIntire 116
Frank McKee 118
C.G. Merrill 120
H.W. Merrill 122
D.F. Morey 124
John H. Morrell 126
Claude Myers 128

A.H. Nelson 130
Wm S. Otis 132
Henry Phillips 134
M.W. Poling 136
George Potter 138
Jas. F. Powell 140
N.F. Reed 142
Guy N. Reid 144
W.L. Sargent 146
Dan R. Shea 148
F.W. Simmons 150
George B. Simmons 152
D.D. Smith 154
J.J. Smith 156
Dr. S.A. Spilman 158
G.F. Spry 160
R.L. Stenz 162
Roy E. Stevens 164
Theo A. Stoessel 166
James Swirles 168
C.R. Tower 170
W.S. Vinson 172
Frank Von Schrader 174
H.L. Waterman 176
J.N. Weidenfeller 178
H.C. Williams 180
Wm. T. Wilson 182
W.T. Wilson 184
W.B. Wycoff 186
Geo. A. Zika 188

Who's Missing? 190
About the Author 191
Sources 191
Index 192

A Note from the Editor

The 91 caricature drawings in this book have been reproduced as they appeared in the Ottumwa *Courier* between late October 1913 and early March 1914.

The poems which accompanied each drawing were difficult to read in the original print, so they have been recreated here; each is faithful to the first publication.

Information about each man's business, personal interests, family and residence have been added to provide context to the drawings, as have additional illustrations where available. In this book, profiles are presented alphabetically rather than in the random order in which they originally appeared in the newspaper.

Addresses and personal information are listed here exactly as each individual's entry appears in McCoy's Ottumwa City Directory of 1913-1914. This occasionally leads to confusion when compared with other sources, as in the case of Bernard (also called Bernhard) Hofmann, or Mrs. Bernard Hofmann who is listed in various sources under three distinctly different names even though all three clearly refer to the same person. Where such confusion exists I have attempted to include all variations.

Photographs of Ottumwa at the turn of the century are courtesy of the Lemberger Collection. Unless otherwise identified, portraits of individuals appeared in Waterman's *History of Wapello County, Iowa*, published in the same year as the caricatures. Other portraits are from other Wapello County histories or from newspaper microfilm and scrapbooks of newspaper clippings, including obituary notices, mostly dating from the 1930s. The quality of these images is regrettably low. In these cases specific dates are sometimes not available, and as with today's obituaries, a photo may have been years old at the time it was published.

Ads are reproduced from the McCoy's Ottumwa City Directory of 1913-1914 and from the Ottumwa *Courier* microfilm of the same years. Both are courtesy of Ottumwa Public Library.

Leigh Michaels

"Some Well Known Ottumwa Men"

From the end of October 1913 until the beginning of March 1914, the Ottumwa *Courier* ran an almost-daily series featuring caricatures of Ottumwa businessmen. More than 90 were featured, each represented by a drawing exaggerating certain physical features, accompanied only by a short and light-hearted poem about the man, his business, his hobbies, or his civic activities. The only headline was **"Some Well Known Ottumwa Men."** There was no introductory article when the series started, and nothing was said in the newpaper about the inspiration for the series or the expected scope or duration of the feature.

There was no explanation of how the 91 men were chosen — and there are examples of prominent Ottumwa men of the era who were not included. The drawings appeared in a seemingly random order — not alphabetical, and not organized by industry or by geographical area within the city.

Though in this era -- eighteen months after the sinking of the *Titanic* and six months before the start of World War I in Europe -- a number of businesses in Ottumwa were headed by women, no women were included in this series. Only one of the wives from this list of 91 men was deemed worthy of a listing separate from her husband's in the city directory that year.

Nothing is known of the artist. Several of the drawings have small initials tucked into unobtrusive corners where an artist would be likely to sign his work. In each case where they appear, the initials are different. But the style of the drawings is so similar that it would seem impossible for them to be the work of multiple artists, so the initials are unexplained.

Caricature has been a popular form of art for hundreds of years; Leonardo da Vinci was an early caricaturist. The word comes from the Italian *caricare*, meaning to change or load. By changing and exaggerating some features, the artist can either flatter or lampoon his subject — mocking with gentle humor or with vicious wit. The most common use of caricature in the modern day is in editorial cartoons; the traditional pairing of caricature drawings with newspapers has endured for well over 100 years.

Unlike many editorial cartoons, this set of caricatures of businessmen does not hold them up to ridicule. But more than a century after their creation, the drawings still bring light and personality to 91 men who were prominent in the economic and civic affairs of Ottumwa. They were the movers and shakers of their time.

Lucius A. Andrew

Occupation: President, Citizens Savings Bank
Business address: Second, corner of Market
Wife: Hazel I. Andrew
Residence: Prairie Avenue north of Carter Avenue

L. A. Andrew was state superintendent of banking for the State of Iowa as well as president of the Citizens Savings Bank of Ottumwa. During the Depression, he was responsible for receiving and approving applications of state banks to reopen after the "bank holiday" of 1933.

Because of financial panic in the early days of the Depression, runs on banks were common and many financial institutions were -- or were feared to be -- insolvent. Days after President Franklin Roosevelt took office in March 1933, he declared a bank holiday. From March 6 to March 10, banking transactions were suspended across the nation, with the sole exception of making change.

1930

When the week was over, banks were allowed to reopen under varying rules depending on their financial condition. Some could only accept deposits, while the healthiest institutions could operate under normal procedures.

The bank holiday was successful. By the beginning of April confidence was largely restored and the crisis was over.

The panic led to the creation of the Federal Deposit Insurance Corporation (FDIC) which still insures depositors.

The photo at right shows L. A. Andrew in his role as state superintendent of banking at the end of the bank holiday, with applications from state banks to be allowed to reopen.

1933

He doesn't like the winter time,
    For nothing grows at all;
He'd rather live those sunny months
    Between the spring and fall;
Then on his Prairie Avenue farm
    He hoes and rakes and sows;
He'd rather raise a winning calf
    Than do anything else he knows.

William T. Archer

Occupation: Manager Pacific Mutual Life Insurance Co.
Secretary / treasurer American Commercial Travelers Association
Business address: 102 E. Main
Wife: Clara S. Archer
Residence: 409 W. Second

WILLIAM T. ARCHER

William T. Archer, manager for Southern Iowa for the Pacific Mutual Life Insurance Company of Los Angeles, was also secretary-treasurer of the American Commercial Travelers Accident Association. He was born in La Plata, Missouri, in 1863. He worked in a number of industries and professions, including railway postal clerk, baker, railroad ticket agent, and traveling salesman of farm equipment, before turning to the life insurance business in 1904.

He married Clara S. Kraner of Ottumwa and they had five children. Archer was a Republican and a member of the Episcopal Church.

"He is easily approachable and is never too busy to be courteous nor too courteous to be busy." -- Waterman, 1914.

The Family Needs It

The Pacific Mutual Life Insurance Co.

PROVIDES PERFECT PROTECTION

W. T. ARCHER, Manager

New Phone 84   OVER OTTUMWA SAVINGS BANK

Leigh Michaels

The pace he now sets is terrific,
Says the insurance you want is "Pacific";
    Never thinking of pay,
    He works night and day,
And the growth of his list is prolific.

John T. Bohe

Occupation: Stentz & Bohe (cigar manufacturers)
Business address: 215 E. Main
Wife: Isadore M. Bohe
Residence: Alta Vista Avenue near city limits

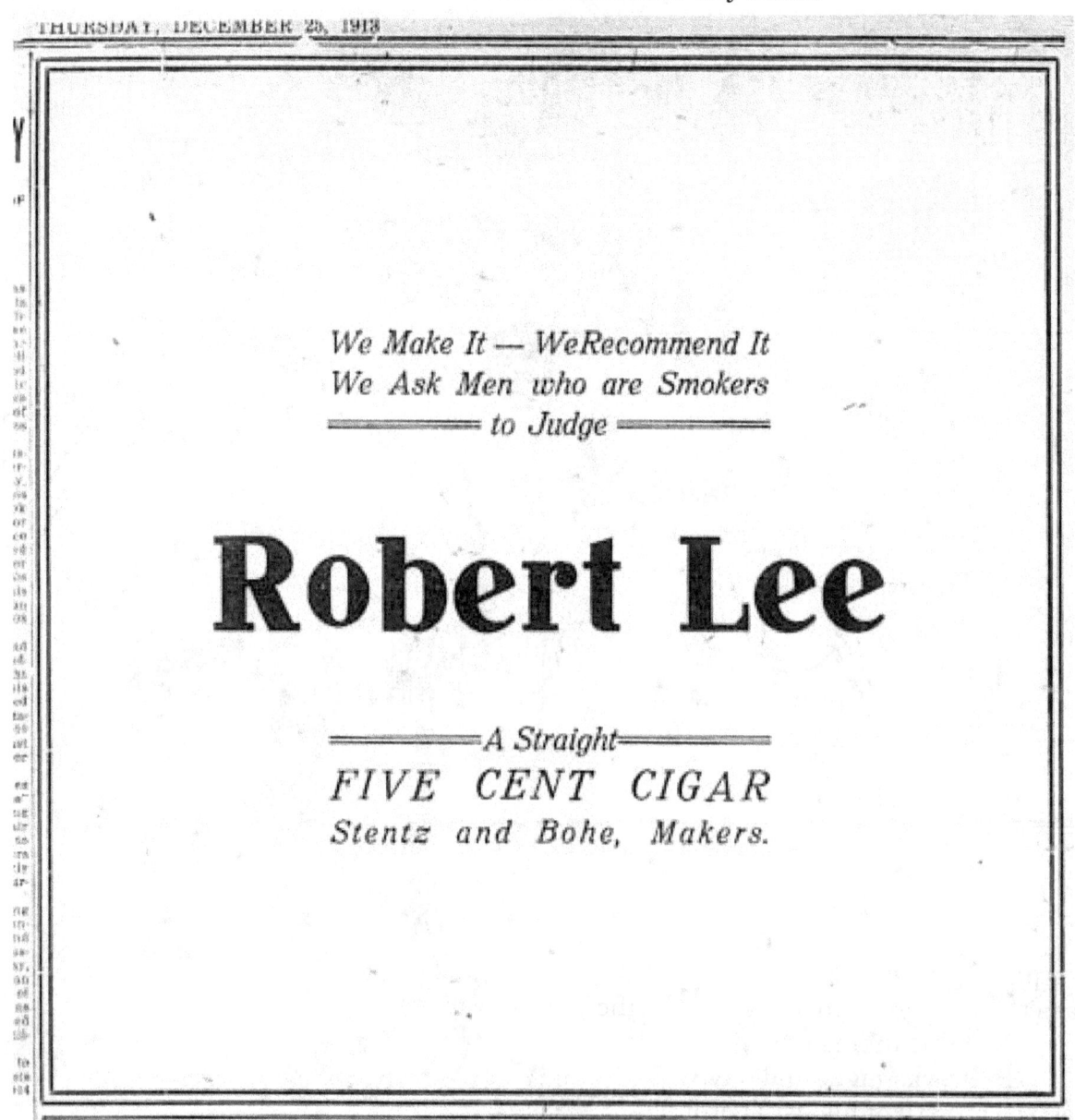

Ad for Robert Lee cigars from the 1913 Ottumwa *Courier*.
The firm of Stentz & Bohe also made the Little Ben cigar.

This pleasant man you now do see
Is one of the makers of the Robert Lee,
    It's 5 cents straight, as good as ten,
    Its only rival is Little Ben --
These two cigars sell right on sight,
They're the best that's made, that's honor bright.

So few rhymes for Browning!
    It might perhaps be "crowning!"
Or we could make it "downing!"
    But for him it can't be "frowning!"

J. Dean Browning

Occupation: Purchasing Agent Dain Manufacturing Co.
Business address: Vine corner of Madison
Wife: Juliet F. Browning
Residence: 328 E. Fourth

Joseph Dain began manufacturing hay harvesting equipment in Missouri in the 19th century and moved the factory to Ottumwa in 1900, building a facility on Vine Street at the corner of Madison Avenue. In 1910 the company was acquired by John Deere and Company. The plant operated under the title of the Dain Works until 1947 when it became known as John Deere Ottumwa Works.

J. Dean Browning had been cashier, bookkeeper, and traffic manager for Dain Manufacturing, working for the company since about 1905. By 1913 he had been promoted to purchasing agent for the Dain Works.

Dain Manufacturing Company hay loader, built in Ottumwa between 1900 and 1910. Machinery to gather the hay and push it onto the wagon was an enormous saving in time and labor for farmers. The company's hay-loading products were a major reason why the company was acquired by John Deere & Co. in 1910.

Leon R. Clausen

Occupation: Secretary and General Manager, Dain Manufacturing Co.
Business address: Vine corner of Madison
Wife: Agnes Clausen
Residence: 116 N. Union

L. R. Clausen came to Ottumwa about 1913, after the merger of John Deere & Co. with Dain Manufacturing, to take up a position as general manager of what became known as the Dain Works. The Dain Works produced hay-making equipment including a revolutionary side-delivery rake and hay loader. Before the production of equipment of this type, haying -- turning the drying grass, loading wagons in the field and unloading into the barn -- was entirely done by hand.

Dain Manufacturing Company, forerunner of John Deere Ottumwa Works

Leigh Michaels

When asked their choice to make,
Of hay press, mower or rake,
    The farmers decide
      "A Dain is our pride,
It's tested, we know it won't break."

Seneca Cornell

Occupation: Lawyer; Partner Cornell Rental Agency
Business address:
1-2 I.O.O.F. Building, 104 N. Court
Wife: Clara E. Cornell
Residence: 524 W. Fourth

In 1914 Seneca Cornell had been an attorney for 32 years. He was born in 1858 in Jefferson County and raised on a farm there before being educated at Parsons College in Fairfield. He had to suspend his education at the age of 20 due to the temporary failure of his eyesight. When he had recovered sufficiently, he began reading law -- the usual practice in the days before law schools became common -- with the Honorable James F. Wilson, a United States Senator, at Fairfield. He was admitted to the bar in 1882. He practiced law in Eldon until 1891 when he moved to Ottumwa to conduct a general law practice.

He served as Wapello County attorney for six years, running as a Democrat, and during his time in office he was responsible for trying John Junkins, the murderer of Clara Rosen, who was assaulted on February 5, 1909 while she was walking to the home of her sister. Rosen died of blunt force injuries to the head. Junkins was arrested after pawning the diamond from Rosen's engagement ring; he confessed and directed detectives to where he had discarded the ring itself and where he had hidden the other jewelry taken from Rosen. After months in various jails -- where he was both threatened by vengeful mobs and visited by infatuated women -- Junkins was tried in Centerville, found guilty and sentenced to death. He was hanged at the Iowa State Penitentiary in Fort Madison on July 29, 1910.

Cornell married Clara E. Caster, a daughter of Dr. Paul Caster, and they had one son. Cornell was a member of the International Order of Odd Fellows, Knights of Pythias, and Benevolent Protective Order of Elks. He was a Presbyterian.

"His life along many lines has proven one of usefulness and worth, and the majority of those who know Seneca Cornell entertain for him warm regard and respect." --Waterman, 1914.

> This firm looking man's name is Cornell,
> What he is thinking you seldom can tell.
> From Blackstone he makes notes,
> But knows all about boats,
> And his fish stories sure ring the bell.

William N. Cramblit

Occupation: Cramblit and Poling (clothing)
Business address: 132 E. Main
Residence: 101 N. Hancock

Cramblit & Poling was a fairly new business in 1913, celebrating its third anniversary during the Christmas season. Note the typo in the header.

If you wish to be treated fair,
    And you want to be well groomed,
You'll find his dealings are on the square,
    And his smile is never assumed.

The grandstand seat is just a board,
But that was forgotten when the home team scored.
Still Frank will contend
When the game's at an end,
The Penn is mightier than the sword.

Frank B. Cresswell

Occupation: General agent, Cresswell & Grube
Penn Mutual Life Insurance
Business address: 132 E. Main
Wife: Emma Cresswell
Residence: 117 N. College

By 1914, Frank B. Cresswell had been general agent and representative of the Penn Mutual Life Insurance Company in southeastern Iowa for nearly 30 years. A native of Van Buren County, he was born in 1858 and moved to Ottumwa in 1877, working as a clerk in various stores. He became involved in the fire insurance business in 1883 and within a few years was named general agent. The partnership of Cresswell & Grube sold fire insurance.

He married Emma F. Scott and they had one son. A Republican and a Mason, he was also involved in the Ottumwa Pickle Company. Along with Charles Greenleaf Merrill he owned controlling interest in the City Savings Bank and had various other banking interests including the Iowa Savings Bank and banks in Albia, Chillicothe, Agency and Chicago.

The 100 block of East Main about 1905, looking toward Court Street from Market and Main. Cresswell & Grube would have been about halfway down the block on the left.

Lee T. Crisman

Occupation: Secretary / treasurer L. T. Crisman Co.
planing mill, contractors / builders
Business address: 138-140 Church
Wife: Bertha Crisman
Residence: 174 N. Ward

A native of Illinois, L. T. Crisman came to Ottumwa in 1886 at the age of 20 to prospect for coal for the Hawk Eye Coal Co. Later he became involved with carpentry work and contracting. In 1899 he purchased the planing mill at 314 W. Main which became known as the Ottumwa Mill & Construction Co. He was also involved in Ottumwa Brewing & Ice Co. before returning to the contracting and building business, incorporating in 1907 as the L. T. Crisman Co. The company manufactured mill work, store fixtures, bank fixtures, etc. He served on the city council in 1910 but was no longer on the council by 1913.

A Democrat, he was a Mason and also belonged to the Benevolent Protective Order of Elks, Royal Arcanum, Eagles, and Woodmen of the World.

L. T. CRISMAN CO. 138-140 CHURCH ST.
Old Phone 3214
New Phone 386-R

GENERAL CONTRACTORS AND BUILDERS

Heavy Concrete, Brick and Iron Work a Specialty

No contract is too large for Lee,
    And nary a one too small.
He'd build a fancy chicken coop,
    Or tackle the pyramids tall.

Frank Ladd Daggett

Occupation: Undertaker and Embalmer, E. Daggett & Sons
Business address: 126 W. Second
Wife: Leora Daggett
Residence: 116 N. Wapello

Frank L. Daggett, manager of the family firm of undertakers, was born in Ottumwa in 1874. He married Maud Leora Sprague, who was also a graduate of the Hohenschuh-Carpenter Embalming School in Iowa City where Daggett was trained, and they worked together in the business. They had four children of whom only one survived to adulthood.

Daggett was active in the Masonic lodge, Odd Fellows, and Modern Woodmen, along with many other fraternal organizations. He was active in the YMCA, and he belonged to the Methodist Episcopal Church. He served terms as president of the State Funeral Directors Association and of the sixth district of Iowa funeral directors.

"Theirs is an attractive and hospitable home, and its good cheer is greatly enjoyed by their many friends." --Waterman, 1914.

He died in April 1931 at the age of 56 following a stroke. He had been in the funeral business for 30 years and at the time of his death was a partner with Seth Barker in the firm known as the Daggett Funeral Service.

1931

> Old Father Time is sure at last
>   To get us one and all;
> When that last day for you arrives,
>   This is the man to call.
>
> From cares so serious as these
>   One surely needs a rest;
> Frank gets his as he ought to do,
>   By singing at his best.

Wallace Rosecrans Daggett

Occupation: President, Iowa Steam Laundry
Business address: Market corner of Third
Wife: Marie Daggett
Residence: 322 E. Fifth

In addition to being head of Iowa Steam Laundry, Wallace R. Daggett was involved in banking, following his father's footsteps at the Iowa National Bank. He was educated at Andover, Massachusetts and Poughkeepsie, New York, and learned the banking trade in Kansas, North Carolina, and Arkansas before returning to Ottumwa in 1895. He was also involved with Janney Manufacturing, which built agricultural implements. He was Republican and Episcopalian and had served the city as an alderman.

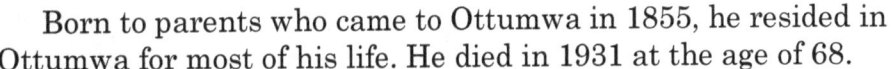

Born to parents who came to Ottumwa in 1855, he resided in Ottumwa for most of his life. He died in 1931 at the age of 68.

> To look at this man
>   you never would think
> He'd had your shirt marked
>   with indelible ink.
> There's not a machine
>   in the house that will tear 'em
> While he's at the club
>   playing three cushion carrom.

About 1930

Movers & Shakers

John says that the hens are too slow,
Don't lay enough eggs, don't you know;
   He's not a price cutter,
   He buys lots of butter,
And of cocks he sells all but the crow.

30

John B. Dennis

Occupation: J. B. Dennis Co. (butter, eggs, poultry)
Business address: 218-220 Tisdale
Wife: Brehilda Dennis
Residence: 329 W. Fifth

At the turn of the century, John B. Dennis was a partner in the firm of Samuel Lilburn & Co., packers and shippers of butter and eggs.

Samuel Lilburn of St. Louis started the business in 1872, with offices at the corner of Second and Green streets, in a building which later was the home of the Benevolent Protective Order of Elks. (The building burned in 1968, when it housed the Eagles club, and was replaced.) Lilburn soon became known as "The Butter King of the West," supplying markets in Philadelphia, New York, Boston and San Francisco.

After Lilburn's death in 1888, the business was operated by A. W. Johnson. In 1889 John B. Dennis purchased an interest. In 1901 the company was still operating under the Lilburn name, but by 1913 it had moved and was renamed for the new owner.

John B. Dennis was born in Missouri in 1853 and came to Wapello County with his parents in 1864. He was educated at the Quincy Commercial College in Quincy, Illinois, and worked in the First National Bank in Ottumwa until purchasing an interest in the Lilburn company. An independent Democrat, he served as deputy county auditor. He was a director of the Ottumwa National Bank and a promoter of the Wapello Savings Bank. He married Brehilda Bedwell in 1883.

John B. Dennis home, 329 W. 5th Ottumwa, Iowa   before Dec. 1899

J. Fred Dings

Occupation: Grocer
Business address: Grocery, 402 W. Second;
meat market, 406 W. Second;
flour and feed, 111 S. Wapello
Wife Caroline Dings
Residence: 312 W. Fourth

The interior of J.F. Dings Grocery, taken about 1911. Among the many interesting aspects are the baskets of potatoes and turnips, a display of cigar boxes in the showcase at left, the workers' aprons and hats, and the elevated office area at center right. Many grocery items were shelved behind the counter, where clerks would wait on customers. The sign at right announces the new Dings meat market, which had just opened in the next storefront.

Leigh Michaels

He's young in years, though long ago
    He centuries had made
On this good wheel with naught at all
    But his own strength for aid.

He still is racing o'er country roads,
    On longer trips by far;
For the bike of old hath given place
    To a great big touring car.

William J. Donelan

Occupation: W. J. Donelan and Co. (dry goods, cloaks, suits, millinery, carpets, shoes, men's furnishings)
Business address: 121-123-125 E. Main
Wife: Theresa Donelan
Residence 424 W. Fourth

By 1901 the Donelan's store was considered the most complete dry-goods store in Wapello County. William J. Donelan, a native of Ireland, worked for Macy's Department Store in New York when he first arrived in the United States, moving on to St. Louis before coming to Ottumwa. A Catholic, he was also a member of the Benevolent Protective Order of Elks.

about 1930

"Qualties That Tell, At Prices That Sell" Have Made

Donelan's
W. J. DONELAN & COMPANY

Ottumwa's Biggest, Best and Busiest Store

We Show The Best For Less In

DRY GOODS

Ready-to-Wear, Millinery, Shoes, Men's Furnishings Trunks, Bags and Suit Cases

1901

This dignified merchant of tone,
Went to Castle of Blarney alone;
But instead of a kiss
Said: "I'll not go amiss" --
And bit a chunk out of the stone.

James K. Dysart

Occupation: President and treasurer, Dysart & Pearson Inc. (clothing and furnishings)
Business address: 203 E. Main and 116 S. Market
Wife: Lucy D. Dysart
Residence: 530 N. Green

> Here's a man who is active and up-to-date;
>   And he's progressive, too.
> In business and politics, nation and state,
>   He often has proven this true.
> He can furnish your clothes from collar to boot,
>   The best to be had, at that;
> You drop in for a necktie, he sells you a suit,
>   And doesn't forget the hat.

Dr. Edward Tyler Edgerly

Occupation: Physician
Secretary / Treasurer J.W. Edgerly & Co. (wholesale druggists)
Business address: 25 Hofmann Building; 120-124 W. Main
Wife: Nettie T. Edgerly
Residence: 319 E. Fifth

Dr. E. T. Edgerly was one of the leading physicians in southern Iowa. One of seven children of Dr. J. W. Edgerly, he was educated at Phillips Exeter academy and Harvard, then graduated from medical school at the forerunner of Northwestern University in 1889. He served his internship at Cook County Hospital in Chicago, after ranking first in the competitive examination for the position. He taught pathology at Northwestern University.

In 1894 he accompanied his father on a trip to Europe, and in Paris Dr. J. W. Edgerly died. Dr. E. T. Edgerly left his practice in Chicago and moved to Ottumwa to become associated with his father's firm, J. W. Edgerly & Co. In 1908 he took up the practice of medicine in Ottumwa.

In 1912, he was commissioned a first lieutenant in the medical reserve corps of the United States Army, entering the service in spite of defective eyesight which he had feared might bar him.

He served as medical director of Sunnyslope tuberculosis sanitarium and was official adviser of the United States veterans' bureau in Ottumwa.

He married Nettie Thurston in 1891. The couple had two children.

He died at age 67 in Rochester, Minnesota following an operation at the Mayo Clinic to remove gall stones. His condition was complicated by a kidney inflammation leading to heart failure.

Here's to the genial medicine man!
    When he hears the call "come quick!"
His army job does not interfere
    With his rushing to the sick.

Movers & Shakers

City property always he has on hand,
He writes insurance to beat the band.
   If you have money he'll detect it,
   If you owe rent he'll collect it --
That's why the whole town knows his stand.

Harry L. Edmunds

Occupation: Real estate and fire insurance
Business address: 116 E. Main
Wife: Ola K. Edmunds
Residence: 220 Albany

Harry L. Edmunds was born in Great Britain in 1872 and came with his parents to Wapello County in 1884. He was educated at Ottumwa Commercial College and then purchased an insurance agency where he made a specialty of fire insurance, along with his real estate interests.

He married Ola Kitterman. He was a Democrat, a member of Trinity Episcopal Church, and a member of the Country Club.

The 100 block of East Main, looking east from Court Street about 1900. Ten years after this view, Harry Edmunds' real estate and insurance office was located at right.

Elmer E. England

Occupation: General manager, Ottumwa Telephone and Electric
Business address: Telephone Building 114-116 W. Second
Wife: Jane England
Residence: 135 E. Maple Avenue

The Girls at the Switchboard

Those young women whose voices you hear calling "Number?" are important personages in telephone affairs.

It is the patient, courteous "Central" girl who makes it possible to increase the joys of living, facilitates the activities of business and who summons help in cases of extremity.

A Human Element

It is the operator who applies intelligence to a machine that never stops — the Human Element that acts to control the wires as they summon aid in times of disaster, calls the doctor in illness or accident, or connects subscribers for a friendly, social chat.

Courtesy and consideration in dealing with these girls will make it easier for them to give better service to all.

IOWA TELEPHONE COMPANY

(Left and right) Though these ads from 1913 were placed by the Iowa Telephone Company rather than Ottumwa Telephone and Electric, they reflect the much different stage of the industry 100 years ago.

No matter wherever you go,
You cannot escape his "Hello,"
    He knows all about volley,
    To beat him is folly,
For he'll play you again, don't you know.

Movers & Shakers

His amperage is enormous
    And his voltage very high,
His mental arc is blinding--
    There's induction in his eye.

When he's after business and
    He starts in its direction,
Electric light is sure to make
    A mighty good connection.

Charles E. Fahrney

Occupation: Acting Manager, Ottumwa Railway & Light Co.
Business address: 201-205 E. Second
Wife: Helen E. Fahrney
Residence: 104 E. Court

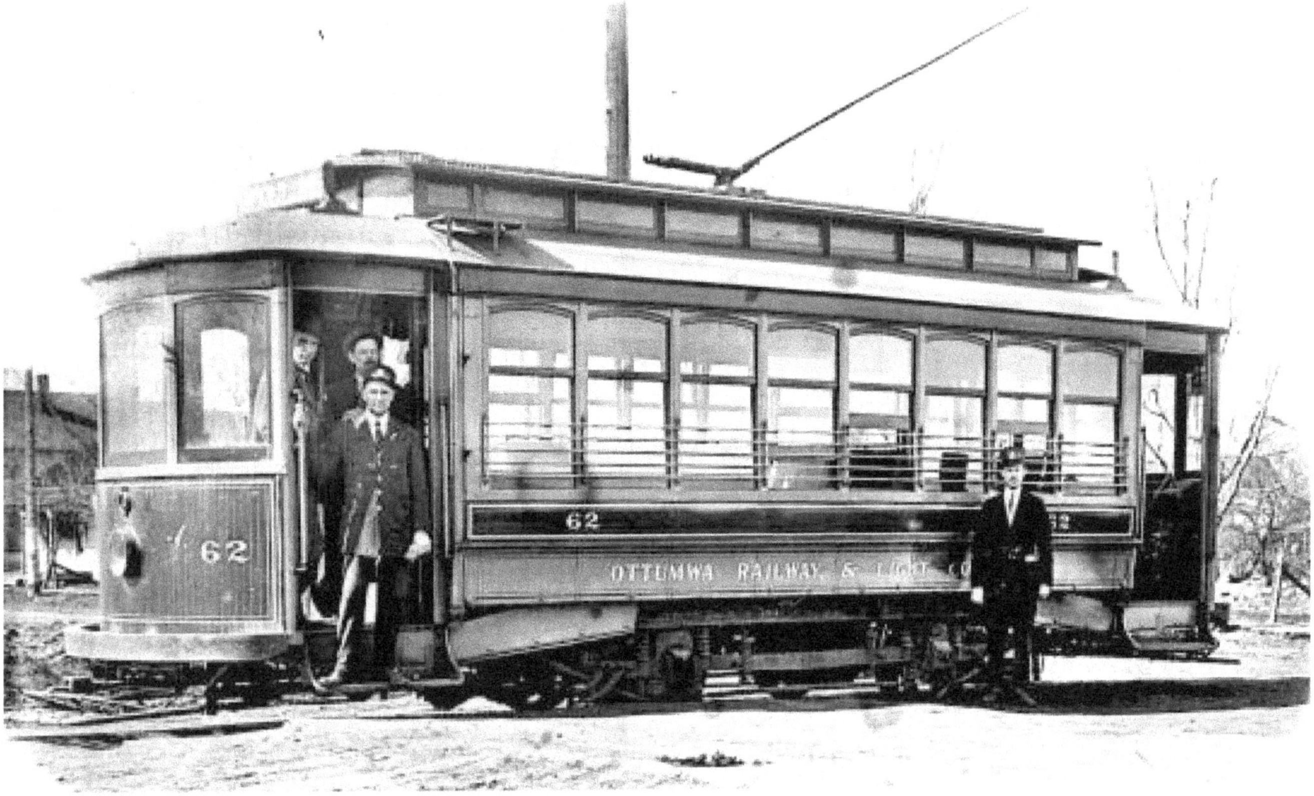

After Charles E. Fahrney's death, his wife Helen established a fund in his memory to provide scholarships for Wapello County students, a program which continues to this day. Residents of Wapello County who are undergraduate or graduate students enrolled full time in Iowa universities and colleges can apply.

The maximum value of each scholarship is currently $1,500. More than 3000 scholarships worth more than $6.5 million have been awarded to date.

Julius Fecht

Occupation: Cigar manufacturer
Business address: 212 S. Jefferson
Residence: 137 N. Washington

Ottumwa's best known cigar manufacturer, Julius Fecht arrived in 1874 to work as a cigar maker, opening his own shop in 1884. Until 1895 he was a partner with his brother Emil Fecht, and they produced up to one million cigars annually. In 1914 the factory was located on South Jefferson, but later Julius Fecht built the multi-story factory building which still stands on the southwest corner of Main and Marion.

The cigar industry operated into the 1920s, and Fecht employed as many as 35 people, mostly women, to turn imported tobacco into cigars by hand. He was also a partner in a tobacco-growing operation in Cuba, allowing him to better control costs by eliminating the middleman.

Leigh Michaels

The wind may blow, the storm may rage,
    The elements run wild,
Just give him a boat, a reel and a hook,
    He's happy as a child --
But all his time's not spent in play,
    As our green parks will prove,
Ottumwa or Cuba, at home or abroad,
    He's always on the move.

William Fiedler

Occupation: Vice-president, Harper & McIntire Co.
Business address: wholesale hardware 216-222 Commercial
retail hardware, stoves, tinware, plumbing 105 E. Main
Wife: Belle Fiedler
Residence: 205 W. Fourth

William Fiedler managed the retail arm of Harper & MacIntire, located at 105 E. Main. He was born in Pennsylvania in 1860 and the family moved to Wapello County a year later. His father was an architect, engineer, and superintendent of construction. William started with Harper & MacIntire as an office boy at the age of eighteen and worked his way up. The business was one of the most extensive commercial enterprises in Ottumwa.

He married Belle Graves and they had four children. He was a member of the First Methodist Episcopal Church, Masons, Wapello Club and Ottumwa Country Club.

Leigh Michaels

His ancestors were noted men,
    For lineage and learning;
Why, Nero was a Fiedler when
    All ancient Rome was burning.

Thomas Dove Foster

Occupation: Chairman, board of managers John H. Morrell & Co. Ltd.
Business address: Iowa Avenue and Hayne
Wife: Eliza J. Foster
Residence: 205 E. Fifth

T. D. Foster was involved with Morrell & Co. from 1865 onward, first in Castlecomer, County Kilkenny, Ireland, then in Liverpool, England, New York, and Ottumwa, where the company was headquartered. Born in England in 1847, he was the son of William Foster and Mary Morrell Foster.

He married Eliza M. Thompson in 1872; after her death in 1879, he married Eliza J. McClelland in 1885.

Two of his sons -- Thomas Henry Foster and George McClelland Foster -- went on to be involved with the Morrell company.

He was a member and steady supporter of the East End Presbyterian Church, which was established and located near the Morrell plant for the convenience of workers.

In Birmingham and Rotterdam,
    In Portland and in Macon,
In Singapore and St. Paul, too,
    They eat his hams and bacon.

Edward D. Fowler

Occupation: President, Fowler & Wilson Coal Co.
President, Alpine Coal Co.
Business address: Leighton Building
Wife: Laura C. Fowler
Residence: 218 Oakwood Ave.

FIND COAL VEIN FIVE FEET THICK

NEW MINES AT BIDWELL BID FAIR TO BECOME GOOD SIZED MINING CAMP.

The Bidwell Coal Co., has reached coal in its new shaft at Bidwell and the vein runs to a thickness of five feet and ten inches and is very gratifying to the operators of the new mining venture. The opening of the mine adds another to the several coal industries adjacent to Ottumwa. The outlook for the new venture is very bright as the men in charge are well known Illinois and Iowa mine operators and are familiar with coal mining in its every phase.

The intention is to develop the field which in extent runs from 400 to 600 acres under which is laid a good strata of coal. The men in charge are reticent as to making predictions beyond the merest statement regarding the prospects for their new mine. They say that the out-put when the mine is underway will be 1,000 tons gross daily. As the property develops it is expected to make a mining camp at Bidwell that will bring hundreds of people to that locality.

In 1901, nearly a quarter of a million tons of coal were extracted in Wapello County.

The Alpine Coal Company had been in business since at least 1865, with a large mine located at Alpine Station, two miles below Cliffland, where the seam was from four to five feet thick.

None of the mines in the county were more than 130 feet deep.

Coke is a solid fuel made by heating coal in the absence of air, so that volatile components are driven off. Coke has a higher carbon content and few impurities, making it a superior fuel source.

"Rathbun Block" was a brand name for a specific type of coal, probably based on size of the pieces.

1913 Ottumwa *Courier* story announcing the discovery of a new coal vein in Wapello County. Bidwell is about eight miles west of Ottumwa and lies north of Highway 34.

He is indeed a hustler,
    Knows how to take a knock;
But his troubles all are over
    Since he's selling "Rathbun Block."

Nathan Friedman

Occupation: The Big Store (dry goods, clothing, shoes, furniture, stoves, etc.)
Business address: 108-110 E. Main
Wife: Bertha Friedman
Residence: 318 N. Washington

Leigh Michaels

He started with a little stock
    And then he got a hunch
To go into the market
    And buy a bigger bunch.

But still he wasn't satisfied;
    Oh yes! he longed for more,
And soon indeed the time arrived
    To buy the great Big Store.

Jarrett Wesley Garner

Occupation: wholesale dry goods
Business address: 222-224 E. Second
Wife: Mary Y. Garner
Residence: 424 E. Second

3. J. W. Garner.
1890

J. W. Garner operated an extensive dry-goods business in Ottumwa, starting as a clerk in the firm of Thomas Devin & Sons in 1858, the year before the first railroad came to Ottumwa. In 1869 the store and inventory were badly damaged by fire, and Garner bought the remainder, which formed the nucleus of his new business. He operated the store under various names and with various partners until 1891 when it became J. W. Garner & Co. By the turn of the century he employed four traveling salesmen and supplied hundreds of stores with wholesale dry goods including notions, underwear and gentlemen's furnishings.

He was one of the original stockholders in the Ottumwa Savings Bank. He also served as treasurer of the Grand Opera House Co., the Ottumwa Artesian Well Co., and the Ottumwa Electric and Steam Power Co.

He was born in Ohio in 1846 and moved with his family to Ottumwa in 1858. He married Mary Y. Yarnell and the couple had six children. An Episcopalian, he was a member of the Wapello Club.

At age 89, his name was submitted to Ripley's "Believe It or Not" as the oldest active dry goods merchant in the United States. He had been in the business for 76 years.

The Wapello Club, located on East Second Street.

Leigh Michaels

He longs for the feel of the flexible reel
    In the swing of a practical cast;
The flop of the fish from the pan to the dish
    Is his joy! Oh, long may it last!

Thomas E. Gibbons

Occupation: Gibbons Grocery
Business address: 911-913 Church
Wife: Melvina Gibbons
Residence: 357 Quincy Ave.

Thomas E. Gibbons was considered the premiere grocer on Ottumwa's south side. A native of Toronto, Canada, he was born in 1856 to parents who had emigrated from Ireland. In 1870 he started working for McCullough & Lilburn, dealers in butter and eggs. After a short while, he moved to Omaha where he was engaged in the same business. He returned to Ottumwa in 1879 and started into the grocery business, operating with various partners and under different names until 1895 when he opened the Gibbons Tea Store at 911-913 Church Street. By 1914 the name had been changed to Gibbons Grocery.

He married Annie Monley, and after her death in 1891 he married Melvina Wallace. He served as alderman of the Fifth Ward of Ottumwa, the first alderman to be elected from the south side of the river. A Catholic, he was a member of the Woodmen of the World and of the National Union.

Gibbons Grocery in about 1890, before Gibbons moved the business to the south side.

There once was another Gibbons:
He earned fame by the "Fall of Rome" --
    But what claim has he
    Over this grocer you see,
Who furnishes supplies for the home?

James T. Hackworth

Occupation: President Ottumwa National Bank
President Wapello County Savings Bank
Treasurer Hardsocg Wonder Drill Co.
Vice president Ottumwa Iron Works
Business address: 134 E. Main
Wife: Sue C. Hackworth
Residence: 822 N. Court

James T. Hackworth's impact on Ottumwa continues to the present day through the Hackworth trust, which helps to fund the Ottumwa Public Library. He was born in Ohio in 1839 and came to Wapello County at the age of six. He graduated from Iowa Wesleyan University in Mt. Pleasant in 1860, read law, and was admitted to the bar in 1861. He practiced for ten years, and for part of that time was also assistant assessor of United States Internal Revenue. In 1872 he joined with Allen Johnston, A. G. Harrow, and J. G. Hutchison in organizing the Johnston Ruffler Co., manufacturing sewing-machine rufflers and employing as many as 500 workers. He was also involved in organizing the Ottumwa Iron Works, which manufactured machinery to produce screws and cutlery, as well as steam engines. He was one of about twenty Ottumwa businessmen who were ac-

tively involved in bringing Dain Manufacturing Co. to the city.

He married Sue C. Kisinger in 1866 and they lived in a house at the corner of North Court and Pennsylvania which remains on the site today, though it is much changed. He was president of the board of trustees of the Ottumwa Public Library from its founding and left a considerable portion of his estate to help fund the library in perpetuity.

J. T. Hackworth's Residence.

Leigh Michaels

Library, churches, buildings and bank!
This man with the serious face
Must surely be put in the very first rank,
In the daily strenuous race.

Movers & Shakers

An able man is here displayed,
    The grocer of the bunch;
Whene'er he gets a thing to do
    He does it with a hunch.
Tho' other men may long to go --
    In other countries roam --
To him the dearest place on earth,
    Is home, sweet home.

Charles Hallberg

Occupation: Manager, Globe Tea Co.
Business address: 216-218 E. Main
Wife: Catherine Hallberg
Residence: 428 N. Jefferson

Charles Hallberg in 1898, from a photo of directors of the YMCA

Charles Hallberg was born in Sweden in 1868 and was educated there until emigrating to the United States in 1886. Upon his arrival he secured a position with the Globe Tea Co. and steadily worked his way upward, purchasing a third interest in the business at the age of 21. By age 30 he held three-fourths of the stock and made the company one of the important commercial interests of Ottumwa and the largest concern of the kind in Iowa.

A director and treasurer of the wholesale grocery firm of J. G. Hutchison Co., he was also a director of the Iowa Savings Bank.

In 1894 he married Catherine Hoglund, and they had four children. Both were active in the Swedish Lutheran Church. Hallberg served on the school board and was a director of the YMCA. Mrs. Hallberg was a member of the board of the Young Women's Christian Association and president of the Home Culture Club.

Clarence S. Harper

Occupation: Vice-president / secretary, Arnold Jewelry & Music Co.
Vice-president Harper & McIntire (hardware)
Business address: 113 E. Main
Wife: Elizabeth Harper
Residence: 311 N. Marion

Clarence S. Harper was deeply involved with public affairs as chairman of the riverfront improvement commission and president of the Ottumwa Chamber of Commerce. He was also a director of the National Wholesale Hardware Association, and was vice-president, and later president, of Harper & McIntire Wholesale Hardware Co., both in Ottumwa and in Cedar Rapids. He was a member of Rotary and the Presbyterian Church.

Born in Ottumwa, he was educated at Parsons College in Fairfield and at Harvard, and worked for a time as managing editor of the Ottumwa *Courier*. He died in 1936.

Jewelry showroom of Arnold Jewelry & Music on East Main Street. The company employed at least 15 people and would make wedding rings while the customer waited. A piano showroom was located at the top of the stairway (center), featuring an extensive collection of sheet music. The business remained open until about 1960 though in later years it moved to South Market Street and focused on jewelry and watch repair.

Leigh Michaels

about 1930

It's in the joyous summer time
    That he is happy, quite;
He rides the river all day long,
    And often in the night.
Since he has that summer home,
    Of heat he has no fear.
The view is grand, the air sublime
    And all are welcome here.

William T. Harper

Occupation: President, J. W. Edgerly & Co. wholesale druggists
Business address: 120-124 W. Main
Wife: Alice B. Harper
Residence: 941 N. Court

1932

J. W. Edgerly & Co. was primarily a supplier of wholesale drugs, but also dealt in paints, oils, glass, and other products. The firm was formed in 1888 as a partnership between William T. Harper's father, also named W. T. Harper, Dr. J. W. Edgerly, and Charles F. Harlan. Harper senior worked in a drug store in Eddyville and later in the drug business of J. L. Taylor & Co. as well as in the linseed oil business.

William T. Harper, Jr. was born in Ottumwa in 1868 and graduated from high school with the class of 1884. He attended Iowa State College for one year and the State University of Iowa for a year. He then joined his father in the linseed oil business until 1890 when he joined J. W. Edgerly & Co. as an invoice clerk, working his way up to being president of the business by 1913.

He married Alice Beamen. Harper was a Republican.

In February 1940, Harper was honored with a dinner marking his 50-year anniversary with J. W. Edgerly & Co. The newspaper story announcing the event said that "Attending will be... male employees of Edgerly & Co. and a number of Ottumwa's leading citizens -- between 50 and 60 in all."

Leigh Michaels

When there's doubt on a question of freight
Go to Will, and he'll tell you the rate.
But out on Court Hill,
This good-natured Bill
Is wrapt up in the hen and her mate.

Movers & Shakers

Albert G. Harrow

Occupation: Vice president Ottumwa National Bank
Vice president Wapello County Savings Bank
Secretary / treasurer The Courier Publishing Co.
Business address: 134 E. Main
Treasurer Ottumwa Iron Works
Wife: Mary C. Harrow
Residence: 433 W. Fourth

A. G. Harrow was born in 1852 in a log cabin on the Harrow farm, located approximately where North Benton and West Fourth streets intersect. He was educated at Iowa State Agricultural College at Ames. He was involved in Johnston Ruffler Co., Ottumwa Iron Works, Ottumwa National Bank, Ottumwa Savings Bank and others. He was president of the Ottumwa Gas, Light, Heat & Power Co. and assisted in establishing the city waterworks. He was a director of Dain Manufacturing and was the largest stockholder, second only to the president; at the time Dain merged with John Deere & Co., he owned more than a fourth of the company's stock.

He married Mary C. Carpenter. A member of the Wapello Club, he served as president.

> He can tell a mighty good story;
>   At a meeting he's never late.
> Another feature about him,
>   He's never forgotten a date.
>
> Should you wish to know when Logan ran
>   Or the birthday of John Jay,
> Harrow is right there every time
>   With the year, the month and the day.

Carl T. Haw

Occupation: Vice president Haw & Simmons Co.
(wholesale hardware)
Business address: 106-108 W. Main
Wife: Nora C. Haw
Residence: 210 Oakwood

Prominently identified for many years with business and civic affairs in Ottumwa, Carl T. Haw died at his home, 210 Oakwood Avenue, of heart failure in August 1930. At the time of his death he was president of the Daggett-Haw Transfer Co.

Haw & Simmons Hardware, after a 1913 fire destroyed at least five buildings housing at least nine businesses in downtown Ottumwa

This elegant picture of Haw,
Shows off to advantage his jaw.
      We admire his pose
         From his boots to his nose;
It's the best one that we ever saw.

Bernard Hofmann

Occupation: building rental
Business address: 33 Hofmann Building, 101 S. Market
Wife: Emma Hofmann
Residence: 314 W. Second

Bernard Hofmann, sometimes referred to as Bernhard Hofmann, was born in Germany in 1843 and worked as a cooper and brewer until moving to the United States, where he spent time in New York and Chicago before arriving in Ottumwa in 1872. He was employed by the Bower & Schaub Brewery company for two years, then embarked in the brewing business on his own until 1890. From then he turned to buying and selling real estate, and in 1893 built the Hofmann Building. The first Hofmann building was destroyed by fire in March 1940 and was replaced by the six-story building which bore the same name and remains at 101 S. Market today.

Mrs. Hofmann is variously identified as Emma (city directory) Mary Rosina and Maria (Waterman, 1914).

Leigh Michaels

He came to Ottumwa in an early day,
"It looks good to me and I believe I'll stay."
      He didn't watch the clock,
        But built an office block,
And bought all the buildings
        that came his way.

Movers & Shakers

Frank P. Hofmann

Occupation: Druggist
Business address: Market corner of Second
Wife: Isabella Hofmann
Residence: 122 W. Fifth

about 1930

Frank P. Hofmann was one of six children born to Bernard Hofmann. He graduated from Northwestern University of Chicago in 1902 and opened a drug store in the Hofmann Building which had been built by his father. He married Isabelle (or Isabella) Matson in 1905 and the couple had two sons, Philip Bernard and Richard Matson (who later operated Hofmann Drug). He belonged to the Wapello Club and the Country Club as well as being a member of the Episcopal Church. He served as president of the Ottumwa Chamber of Commerce and was chairman of the local NRA (National Recovery Administration) compliance board during the Depression.

A soda fountain was a common feature in drug stores, and the fountain at Hofmann Drug was one of the largest and most popular in the region. The pharmacy is located at right.

Hofmann sells pens, pencils and ipecac,
Candies and chocolate and jap-a-lac --
Post cards and paint,
Salts for the faint,
And says, "Satisfaction or money back."

Believe me, gentle reader, here's
A man who's just O.K.:
His record speaks as well for him
As aught that I could say.

Leigh Michaels

Judge Francis M. Hunter

Occupation: Judge, district court
Wife: Bertha S. Hunter
Residence: 603 E. Second

Francis Marion Hunter served 16 years as a district court judge in the second judicial district of Iowa, presiding in the counties of Wapello, Jefferson, Van Buren, Davis, Monroe, Appanoose and Lucas. Elected to the bench in 1910, he served through 1926.

His obituary states, "During that time he became particularly noted for his interest in juvenile matters," whether the children were involved in criminal activities or were physically handicapped. "Using the power of the court, he is said to have sent more crippled children to the University hospital at Iowa City for treatment than any other Iowa judge."

He was also instrumental in the success of the Ottumwa Hospital, where Mrs. Hunter was president of the board, and he furnished two rooms in the hospital (located at that time on East Second).

He was born in a log cabin on the family farm in Van Buren County in 1858. His mother was born in 1835 on a ship as her parents were emigrating from England. He graduated from law school at the University of Iowa and began practice in Denison, Iowa. He later lived in Council Bluffs, where he was clerk of the federal court, before moving to Ottumwa in 1892. He was a law partner of W. H. C. Jaques until he was elected to the bench as a Republican. After four terms as a judge, he returned to the private practice of law in Ottumwa.

At the time the caricatures were drawn, he was married to Bertha S. Hunter, but he later married Myrtle A. Dungan of Chariton. She was superintendent of schools in Lucas County and the couple met because of their mutual interest in child welfare.

He was a member of Trinity Episcopal Church and was a 50 year Mason. He belonged to the Wapello Club, the Country Club, and the Elks.

1936

Yards filled with lumber, he has without number,
    As well as some farms here and there.
But he's happiest by far when he's out in his car,
    Breathing the fresh country air.

Martin B. Hutchison

Occupation: Vice president Union Trust & Savings Bank
President / treasurer M. B. Hutchison Lumber Co.
treasurer Atlas Acetylene Lighting Co.
Business address: 647 W. Second
Wife: Inez Hutchison
Residence: 434 N. Court

M. B. Hutchison Lumber Co.
Dealers In Lumber, Lath, Shingles, Sash, Doors, Roofing
647 W. Second St.   Phones: New 192, Old 616R

Martin B. Hutchison spent a good part of his career in banking, starting as a collector and then bookkeeper for Ottumwa National Bank in Ottumwa, where he settled in 1882 at the age of 22. By 1903 his health was failing, so he resigned his position with the bank and turned to the lumber business, which would allow him to spend more time outdoors. He organized the M. B. Hutchison Lumber Company and eventually created a line of lumberyards throughout southeast Iowa, with headquarters in Ottumwa. He maintained contact with several banks as a director and was a stockholder in the Ottumwa Automobile Co.

A Republican and a Presbyterian, he was also president of the board of education and a director of the Commercial Association.

He married Inez Jordan in 1888, and they had two daughters.

One of the greatest inventions of the the age is *acetylene light*. Its only rival is the sun itself. Modern ingenuity has perfected a method by which houses, grounds, barns, etc., in any vicinity can be lighted as light as day. It is by means of the *Atlas generator* system, the generator itself being entirely outside of the buildings to be lighted, is located in the ground, out of sight and out of the way. The cost is much less than that of any other method of artificial light and, of course, the gas can be used for cooking, ironing, etc., the same as City gas. The equipment is made only by the Ottumwa-Noline Engine & Pump Co, Ottumwa, Iowa, U.S.A.

W. H. C. Jaques

Occupation: Jaques & Jaques (lawyers)
Business address: 107 N. Court
Wife: Florence Jaques
Residence: 343 N. Marion

Captain W. H. C. Jaques received his commission in the Civil War, volunteering for service in 1862 when he was about 21 years old. He enlisted for service as a member of Company D, Nineteenth Iowa Volunteer Infantry, and served with that unit for eighteen months. He then became captain of Company V, Fifty-Sixth United States Colored Troops, and remained with the unit until the close of the war. After the war's end he served with the Army of the Frontier and on staff duty.

In the fall of 1866, Captain Jaques entered Harvard Law School, spending a year there before coming to Ottumwa where he completed his law reading and was admitted to the bar in 1867. In general practice since 1868, he specialized in trials. By 1914 he was the senior attorney in Wapello County, having served at the bar for more continuous years than any other practitioner.

He served as city solicitor for several terms and was deputy collector of internal revenue. As a Democrat, he was his party's candidate for district judge and judge of the state supreme court.

He married Florence Williams, who served many years as president of the Humane Society of Ottumwa. They had three children.

Jacques was a member of the Grand Army of the Republic, the Loyal Legion, the Benevolent Protective Order of Elks, and the Fishing and Hunting Club. He was the president of the Wapello County Bar Association.

His partner in Jaques & Jaques was his son Jo R. Jaques. "Their devotion to their clients' interests is proverbial, yet they never forget that they owe a still higher allegiance to the majesty of the law." -- Waterman, 1914.

6. W. H. C. Jaques.

1890

When working on a case, his mind and soul are in it;
    No time has he for any care-free hike.
A verdict made and entered, he doesn't wait a minute,
    But scoots away for muscallonge and pike.

Allen Johnston

Occupation: President, Johnston and Sharp Manufacturing Co.
("mousetraps and hardware specialities")
President, Johnston Pressed Gear Co.
Business address: "Bashaw ft of River"
Wife: Elizabeth Johnston
Residence: 531 N. Court

Perhaps the best-known of Ottumwa's many inventors was Allen Johnston. By the age of 14 he had displayed both curiosity and inventiveness, observing workers building a frame house and suggesting means to improve the efficiency of their work. He fixed up a small shop in the attic where he spent his leisure time and his spare cash, making a machine to hull hazel nuts, repairing guns and implements, and making silver and gold rings.

He was born in Ohio in 1848 and was seven when the family moved to Wapello County. In 1867 he left the family farm to study dentistry under his older brother, W. T. Johnston, who was also the agent for the Singer sewing machine. The younger brother, more interested in the sale and mechanisms of sewing machines than in teeth, soon directed his attention to improving the machinery. His first invention was an embroidery attachment; the second was a ruffler attachment which automated the process of creating ruffles from fabrics. Initially sold door to door, the invention eventually led to the organization of the Johnston Ruffler Co. in 1872, and by 1892 the business employed 500.

While much of his work involved sewing machines, he also invented machinery to manufacture screws, cutlery, hollow ball bearings, and gears. He was the holder of more than 125 patents in all.

He died in 1930 at the age of 81, at his home after suffering a heart attack, and was buried in Ottumwa Cemetery.

Why' here's the man whose mind did plan
    To make the hollow ball;
When others failed he never quailed,
    And he outstripped them all.
With wand in hand he takes his stand,
    Now watch him! In a trice
There doth appear, when he is near,
    Full many a strange device.

Movers & Shakers

William E. Jones

Occupation: W. E. Jones & Co. (wholesale and retail flour, feed and seeds)
Business address: 307-309-311 W. Main
elevator 101 Tisdale
Wife: Catherine Jones
Residence: 908 W. Second

By 1914, William E. Jones had been a flour, feed, and grain dealer in Ottumwa for almost a quarter of a century. Born in Ohio in 1843, he came to Wapello County with his family in 1849 and settled on a farm which eventually was absorbed in the city limits of Ottumwa. When he reached adulthood he took over management of the family farm, then moved on to the dry goods business in 1869. By 1880 he was involved in the sales of flour, feed, and grain.

He married Catherine Whipple and they had two daughters. A Republican, Jones served as a member of the county board of supervisors for three years, sat on the school board for nine years, and was a member of the First Congregational Church.

> Here is a man who knows the grain
> From all the different zones --
> But after all, what is the use
> Of making rhymes for Mr. Jones,
> Those who know him well are eager to tell
> His praise in the clearest of tones.

W. E. JONES & CO.
307-311 West Main Street

Wholesale and Retail Dealers in
FEED, FLOUR AND GRAIN
Both Phones 119

If insurance you would have
    Go to the Hofmann block
And look up this man Keating
    Who's steady as a rock.
His companies are the best, he says,
    For they've withstood the shocks
Of many years; and he himself
    Is a man who never knocks.

William H. Keating

Occupation: Real estate and insurance
Business address: 3 Hofmann Building
Wife: Delia V. Keating
Residence: 1618 Prairie Avenue

W. H. Keating — Writes Reliable Fire Insurance
AND BONDS OF ALL KINDS
CAREFUL ATTENTION GIVEN TO MAKING FORMS
Always buy what is absolutely safe.
Room 3, Hofmann Building.   Phone New L-404

Thanksgiving Time

—is close at hand, when the president and governor will call upon all good citizens to count their blessings and give thanks for those they enjoy. If you are a customer of mine you can be thankful that your fire insurance is placed with a company of undoubted strength and integrity, and if you should have a fire, the loss will be adjusted in a liberal and broad minded way. No disputing and dickering to avoid payment of just claims where my companies are concerned, and the rates are just as cheap as with others of doubtful credit. See me before your next policy expires.

W. H. Keating

Phone 404-L.   Room 3, Hofmann Bldg.

W. H. Keating — ACCIDENT LIABILITY AND BOILER **Insurance**
Room 3, Hofmann Building.   Telephone New L-404

Thomas F. Keefe

Occupation: Keefe Bros. (contractors)
Business address: 112 S. Green
Wife: Caroline Keefe
Residence: 425 E. Fourth

Thomas F. Keefe started his career as a brick mason, in time becoming a general contractor who built a number of substantial buildings in Ottumwa. A property owner as well as builder, he was an equal partner in owning a half-block of buildings at the corner of Green and Second Streets, occupied by the Iowa Auto Sales Co., the Wardrobe, and the Garrick Theater. He also owned farm land in the county.

Born in 1864 in Keokuk, he moved with his parents to Wapello County in 1879, traveling by covered wagon. In 1894 he married Catherine (or Caroline) Mary Hibler, and the couple had four children. Keefe was a member of the Benevolent Protective Order of Elks. A Democrat, he served as alderman for eleven consecutive years, serving as president of the city council for one term.

After suffering ill health for many years, T. F. Keefe died in 1936 at age 72, after a heart attack. He was buried in Calvary Cemetery after services at St. Mary's church. He had been a resident of Wapello County for 58 years.

1930s

IOWA AUTO SALES COMPANY
AUTO LIVERY AND REPAIRS
102-104-106 South Green Street   Old Phone 777B, New Phone 1429L

He'd make sulky wheels of cement if he could,
He claims it will last longer than wood,
    He likes a fast "hoss,"
    Does this contractor boss,
And he's one of the men who make good.

George M. Kerns

Occupation: Architect
Business address: Electric Building
Wife: Leona G. Kerns
Residence: 155 E. Court

George M. Kerns was a prominent architect in Ottumwa and the surrounding area. Among the buildings credited to him are Stuart (or Stewart) School, the Wapello County Jail next to the courthouse, Ottumwa Hospital located on East Second Street, First Baptist Church, and the federal building which was constructed in 1910 (and now serves as Ottumwa's City Hall).

1931

> Though with dance, golf and picnic he dally,
> When he bowls he takes up the whole alley;
> But his laugh, all allow,
> 'Tis no joke, I avow,
> Is the best to be found in the valley.

Movers & Shakers

He always looks you in the eye
    When thinking of your mortal end;
For well he knows how few there are
    Who leave behind a dividend.
And though he's probed life's secrets well,
    He's never yet become inured
To knowledge of the fools we be
    To keep on dying -- uninsured.

Leonard M. Kidd

Occupation: Superintendent, Metropolitan Life Insurance Co.
Business address: 16 Hofmann Building
Wife: Maude Kidd
Residence: 222 W. Fourth

West Fourth Street, from the intersection with Washington Street. An upscale residential area in 1913 and 1914, this block is now commercial. All the houses pictured here have been removed, replaced by First Presbyterian Church (completed in 1927) and a telephone company building. One of the houses in the row at left was where Leonard and Maude Kidd lived.

Dr. William B. LaForce

Occupation: Physician and Surgeon
Business address: 5-6-7 Fifth Floor Ennis Building
Wife: Carolina LaForce
Residence: 427 W. Fourth

William B. LaForce came from a long line of physicians. He was the son of Dr. D. A. LaForce, who served as mayor of Ottumwa in the 1890s, and two of his three brothers were also doctors.

"Dr. Will" was a physician and surgeon in Ottumwa from 1893 until giving up his practice in 1917 to become a missionary and surgeon in a hospital near Peking [Beijing], China. He was also an instructor at Tsin Hua college near Peking, which was established after the Boxer Rebellion. He remained in China for 12 years, retiring in about 1929. He then settled in Altadena, California, where he became active with Chinese immigrants and in the Oxford Group, a spiritual movement prominent in the 1930s.

1936

He was educated at Northwestern University and studied in Vienna, Austria. While practicing in Ottumwa, he also served as instructor in the Keokuk Medical College at Keokuk, Iowa.

He married Carolina Bousquet. In 1936, he and his wife went to China on behalf of the Oxford Movement. They were returning to the United States aboard the liner *President Lincoln* when the ship encountered a typhoon at sea. Both Dr. and Mrs. LaForce were thrown to the deck; she suffered a broken arm. Dr. LaForce's spine was seriously injured. He died shortly thereafter and was buried at sea midway between Yokohama, Japan and Honolulu, in accordance with his wishes.

LA FORCE WM B, wife Carolina, physician and surgeon 5-6-7 5th fl Ennis Bldg, office hours 10 to 12 a m, 2 to 4 and 7 to 8 p m, phones new 1303, old 158, r 427 W 4th, phones new 661Y, old 305 Red.

City directory listing from 1913-1914, showing Dr. LaForce's office hours (including regular evening hours) and phone numbers. When not in the office, the doctor would have made house calls.

He works hard for the Sunday School,
He's strong in the Y. M. C. A.
    His name is La Force,
    He's a doctor, of course;
That runs in the family, they say.

Edward L. Lambert

Occupation: General Manager, Ottumwa Gas Co.
Business address: 104 W. Main
Wife: Marion Lambert
Residence: 122 E. Maple

Edward L. Lambert was an Ottumwa resident for only two years, arriving in 1912 as the general manager of the Ottumwa Gas Co. He moved on in 1914 to become manager of the Cedar Rapids Gas Co. in Cedar Rapids, Iowa. He left a distinctive legacy in the city, however, for in his two years as head of the local gas company he supervised the building of a new office and new gas works, investing about two hundred thousand dollars in total.

Born in Illinois in 1881, he graduated from Culver Military Academy and joined United Light & Railway Co., headquartered in Grand Rapids, Michigan. He married Marion Courtney in 1907. While in Ottumwa, Lambert belonged to the Wapello Club, the Country Club, the Benevolent Protective Order of Elks and the Masons. He belonged to the Episcopal Church.

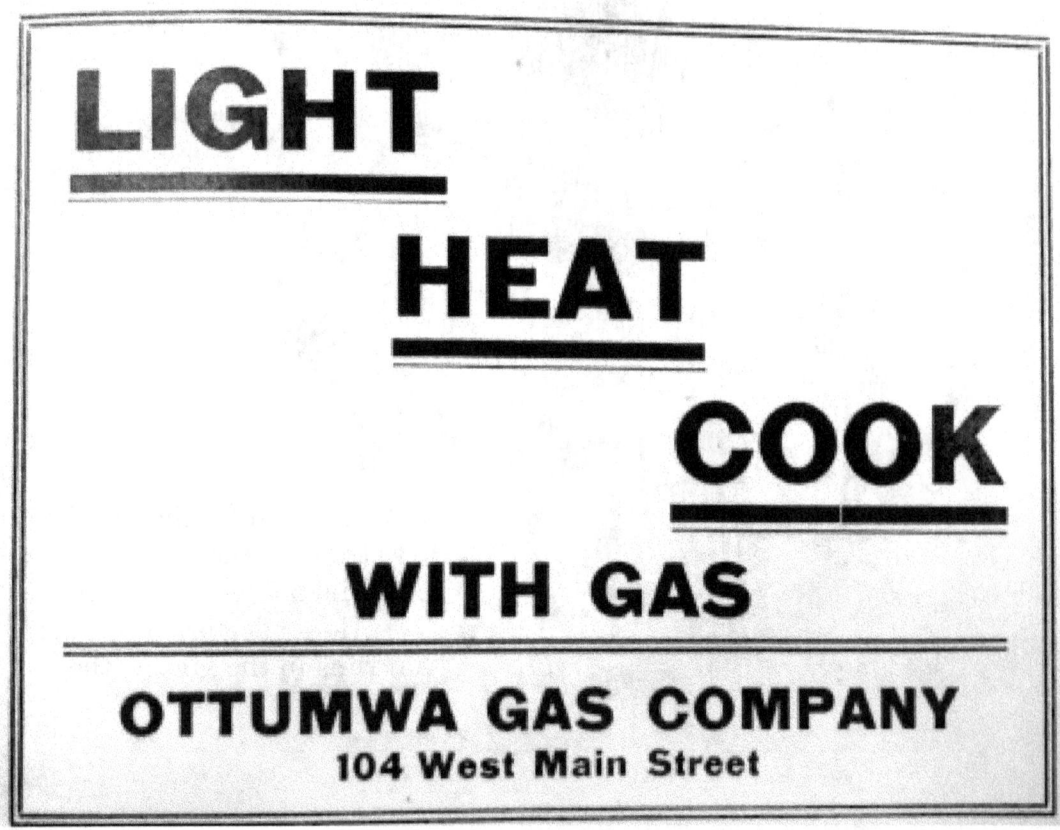

He claims he sells the light that's right,
It makes day out of darkest night --
He hopes it soon will come to pass
That all who eat must cook with gas.

When your hunger's as keen as a knife,
And you don't know what to eat,
Get Mary Jane to save your life,
It's a cinch she can't be beat.

Anton Lowenberg

Occupation: Baker
Business address: 120 E. Second
Wife: B. Elizabeth Lowenberg
Residence: 208 W. Fifth

Brothers Anton and Chris Lowenberg opened their first Ottumwa bakery on South Court Street in 1875, later moving to 120 E. Second and then in the 1920s building a new facility on West Second Street. They were among the first to brand their product, naming their bread "Mary Jane" after the girlfriend of the comic strip character Buster Brown (at the suggestion of Anton's young son Art). The bakery later became synonymous with Sunbeam Bread.

In 1984 the ovens shut down and after 109 years, Lowenberg Bakery ceased blanketing the community with the rich smell of baking bread and frying doughnuts.

The bakery on West Second Street was torn down and the law enforcement center and jail were built on the site.

Lowenberg Bakery at 120 E. Second

Retail store at 120 E. Second

Delightfully Delicious
Mary Jane Bread

Try a loaf of Mary Jane Bread and be convinced of its superiority over others. Get it of your grocer or at

Lowenberg's Bakery
120-122 East Second

> They all believe what he tells 'em;
> If arguments arise he soon fells 'em.
>   No one would walk
>   When he's heard Lytle talk,
> And that is the reason he sells 'em.

Harry J. Lytle

Occupation: Secretary / treasurer Ottumwa Auto Co.
Business address: 313-317 E. Second
Wife: Adeline Lytle
Residence: 932 N. Court

Harry J. Lytle was a partner in the Ottumwa Auto Co., joining the firm in 1909 when he came to Ottumwa. Before focusing on the auto trade, he bought and fed hogs in Mahaska County, later turning his attention to the carpentry trade and then becoming a clerk in a hardware store. He also purchased a moving picture show in Oskaloosa and operated it for eight months.

Ottumwa Auto Co. offered Ford cars and also conducted a wholesale auto supply business, of which Lytle was in charge. He also handled the buying for the firm.

Born in 1882 in Mahaska County, he married Adeline Augustine in 1911. A Presbyterian and a Republican, he belonged to the Wapello Club and the Country Club.

Though Harry J. Lytle's business sold only Fords (above) and did not handle the Maxwell models, the descriptions and prices in this competitor's ad (right) make interesting reading. A 1913 Ford Model T sold for $525, and 170,000 of them were produced that year.

The Maxwell 25 IS HERE
$750 F. O. B. Detroit

A dependable, reliable, high grade 5 passenger car, made by a factory of high standing (37 millions of capital) means that you can't go wrong when you buy a Maxwell 25.

In its first contest the Maxwell 25 wins Mount Falcon hill climb three minutes ahead of the next best. Easily shows heels to many cars of higher power and higher prices.

Call and see it. You will find the following high grade features generally found only in cars of much higher prices.

High tension magneto, selective 3-speed transmission, four semi-elliptic springs, roomy torpedo body, prestolite tank, 30x3½ tires all around, fully equipped, etc.

We also have the following second hand cars in good repair for immediate delivery at the following very low prices, for cash.

One 4-cylinder, Reo 5-Passenger, 30 h. p. Touring Car as good as new............ $350
One 4-cylinder, 30 h. p. Overland $350
One 4-cylinder Maxwell 4-passenger with top and wind shield $250
One 2-cylinder Maxwell Runabout $75
One 4-cylinder, Rambler 5-passenger Touring Car equipped. Run only about 5,000 miles, original price $2000, now............ $500

We also have one Fairbanks-Morse Electric Light plant complete with 6 h. p. Olds special electric engine and switch board with storage batteries, suitable for farm buildings or for a moving picture show outfit, original price $900, now $500

Snow Automobile Co.
315 West Second Street
Ottumwa - - - - - Iowa

James M. Majors

Occupation: Vice president Tower-Majors Candy Co.
Business address: 206 S. Jefferson
Wife: Mabel Majors
Residence: 204 W. Woodland Ave.

A native of Wapello County, James M. Majors was born in 1875 and came to Ottumwa in 1888. When he finished high school in 1892, he joined John H. Morrell & Co. as an office worker. Working his way up, he eventually was transferred to Des Moines where he was manager of the branch house for six years before moving on to Memphis, Tennessee where he stayed for five years. At the end of that time he left Morrell and in 1905 began manufacturing candy in partnership with George B. Simmons and Charles R. Tower as the firm of Tower-Majors Candy. The plant at 206 S. Jefferson employed about 65 people. Tower-Majors was known as the "House of Chocolates" and the brand was known as Perfection Chocolates.

Majors married Mabel Tower, the sister of his business partner Charles R. Tower, and the couple had one son.

> One often wonders why it is
>   Ottumwans are so sweet,
> And why the smile upon the face
>   Of everyone you meet.
> But here's a fact that's not denied,
>   The explanation's dandy,
> The whole town is well supplied
>   With Tower-Majors candy.

Calvin Manning

Occupation: Manning & Wellman (real estate)
Business address: 4-5 Phoenix Trust Building, 114 S. Market
Wife: Juliet Manning
Residence: 720 N. Court

Calvin Manning's name was synonymous with progress in Ottumwa. As secretary of the Coal Palace Association he was instrumental in the building of the Coal Palace exhibit hall in 1890.

A graduate of Cornell University and of the law school at the University of Iowa in 1872, he was city attorney for several years. He was also a legal advisor for businesses including the Iowa National Bank, where he was president for fifteen years.

Born in 1851 in Keosauqua, he was married to Juliet K. Blake in 1877. She was the daughter of Charles F. Blake, one of the pioneer residents of Wapello County and a founder of Iowa National Bank.

Manning was a member of the city council for four years, was a delegate to the national convention of the Republican party twice, and was appointed United States commissioner to the Paris exposition of 1900 by President William F. McKinley. He was a charter member of the Wapello Club.

Here is a man who knows this life
    In all its different phases,
He can play the game of business strife
    From any of its bases.
As president of the Coal Palace,
    And then our County Fair --
As master of ceremonies any time
    Our Calvin's surely there.

John Brown McCarroll

Occupation: McCarroll Bros. (hardware, stoves, tinware, "hot air furnaces")
Business address: 322 E. Main
Wife: Ida B. McCarroll
Residence: 738 W. Second

Though J. B. McCarroll's business was known as McCarroll Brothers, by 1914 he was the sole owner, selling hardware, stoves, tinware, and sporting goods.

He was born in 1859 in Ohio and came with his parents to Wapello County about 1865, eventually settling in Ottumwa by 1871. His father operated a business selling stoves, and J. B. McCarroll was associated with him in that trade, taking it over with his brother C. T. McCarroll after their father's death. In 1898 they sold out to the firm of Harper & McIntire. A year later, he and his brother took over management of the hardware business operated by another family member. After the death of his brother, J. B. McCarroll purchased the widow's interest in the firm and continued to operate the business alone. By 1914 he had been continuously identified with the hardware trade in Ottumwa for nearly 40 years and was one of the leading merchants of the city. He was twice president of the Iowa Retail Hardware Association.

In 1899 he married Ida B. Amos. They had one surviving daughter. McCarroll was a Republican, a 50-year Mason, and a member of the Knights Templar, and he belonged to the Benevolent Protective Order of Elks. The family practiced Spiritualism.

The McCarroll family was strongly abolitionist in pre-Civil War days, and J. B. McCarroll was named for the famous abolitionist who believed that only armed insurrection could overthrow the institution of slavery in the United States. Only a few months after J. B. McCarroll was born, John Brown was hanged after he led a raid on the Federal Armory at Harpers Ferry, Virginia (now West Virginia).

McCarroll retired from active business in 1934 and sold his store to the Fabritz hardware stores. He died in 1940 in Ottumwa.

1940

"Blast" heaters are indeed superfine;
No others as good, I opine.
  But why think of these
  They're not the whole cheese
When a good game of whist is in line.

Movers & Shakers

Here's a man who is hale and hearty,
His age must be about forty;
Every day without fail,
He attends to the mail,
Our postmaster, Mr. McCarty.

Charles W. McCarty

Occupation: Postmaster
Business address: Federal Building
Wife: Sophia McCarty
Residence: 1606 W. Second

Charles W. McCarty was born in Wapello County in 1864, and was raised on the family farm. At age 17 he became a railroad telegraph operator and was connected with the Rock Island Railroad for nearly a quarter of a century. After acting as cashier in the local freight office, he was elected county auditor in 1906 and continued in public service as auditor until resigning to bcome postmaster of Ottumwa in 1913. A lifelong Democrat, he was appointed by President Woodrow Wilson.

He married Sophia Houk in 1890, and the couple had four children. He belonged to the Presbyterian Church.

Ottumwa's federal building, built in 1910, housed the post office as well as federal courts, judges' chambers, and offices for the Internal Revenue Service and federal highway commission. The building is now Ottumwa's City Hall. The architect was George M. Kerns. The building to the left served as St. Joseph Hospital, headquarters of the Sisters of the Humility of Mary, and Catholic Central High School. The building to the right is Hall Candy Co.

Clarence E. McDaniel

Occupation: Proprietor, Ottumwa Boiler Works
City Councilman, dept. of accounts & finance,
parks and public property
Business address: 215 S. Wapello
Residence: 433 N. Fifth

THE OTTUMWA BOILER WORKS

PACKING
Flax Packing
Asbestos Packing
Hemp Packing
Piston Packing
Sheet Rubber Packing
Asbestos and Rubber Gaskets

—FOR SALE BY—

C. E. McDANIEL

New Phone 29   Old 205-B

C. E. McDANIEL

Headquarters for Compression Tanks and Pumps
We Manufacture Them

FIRE BRICK AND GROUND FIRE CLAY

Heavy Sheet Iron, Boiler Steel, Tubes, Rivets,
Etc., Boiler Fronts, Grate Bars, Iron Pipe and
Castings, Etc., Etc.

SPECIAL ATTENTION GIVEN TO REPAIRING

Brass Goods, Inspirators and Injectors, Jet Pumps, Steam
Pumps, Engineer's Supplies, Belting, Packing, Etc., Etc.

Orders By, Mail, Telegraph or Telephone Promptly Attended To

Every day at the boiler works,
Things run steadily, not by jerks;
'Gene grinds no axes,
He handles the taxes,
And his duty he never shirks.

Ralph T. McElroy

Occupation: Real estate, insurance, and rentals
Business address: 126 E. Main, over Cullen's Dry Goods Store
Wife: Maude McElroy
Residence: 305 Oakwood Avenue

Farm for Sale

Eighty acres of land within 3½ miles of city limits of Ottumwa—small house and improvements. Can sell on easy terms or exchange for city property and give plenty of time on balance. See—

Ralph T. McElroy

Above Cullen's Store, Main Street.
Office Phone, Old, 321-Red; Residence Phone 1280-L; Office Phone, New, 19

IOWA
Farm Lands for Sale
Some Big Bargains

160 acres, well improved, lays good, fine location, splendid soil, a real bargain —only $82.50 per acre.

140 acres, improvements good, close to school, good roads to town, nice surrounding country; well fenced—a bargain, $85 per acre.

Insurance and Real Estate

Ralph T. McElroy

Above Cullen's Store.
Office New Phone 19 Old 321-Red.
Residence 1280-L.

This man sells lots of real estate,
And writes insurance, too;
His proposition clear he'll state
And put it up to you.

Walter Hamilton McElroy

Occupation: Lawyer and abstracts
Business address: 236 1/2 E. Main
Wife: Lucille W. McElroy
Residence: 232 E. Maple

Walter H. McElroy opened his law practice in Ottumwa in 1900, in the same office location where his father, Ebenezer Erskine McElroy, had practiced for nearly 30 years.

He was born in Wapello County in 1878, studied law at the State University of Iowa in Iowa City, and was the youngest member of his class to receive a diploma when he graduated in 1900. He immediately joined his father in practice and continued there after his father's death in 1906. His specialty was real estate law, and he conducted a business in abstracts. He was a director and stockholder in the Citizens Savings Bank.

early 1930s

In 1904 he married Lucille H. Wycoff, and the couple had three children. He was a Republican and a Presbyterian; he served as treasurer of the school board and was a member of the Wapello Club and the Country Club.

In the early 1920s he was instrumental in founding the Boy Scout movement in Ottumwa, and was presented the Silver Beaver award, a high honor for an adult worker in the Scout program, in 1932.

During the Depression, he served as director of a manpower program in Ottumwa as part of President Franklin Roosevelt's "emergency re-employment drive".

"His social, genial nature have [sic] gained for him the warm regard of all with whom he has come in contact." -- Waterman, 1914.

If in your title there's a flaw,
    That flaw he'll surely find,
And he can show you readily
    The records that will bind.

While he's an abstractor of note,
    He's devoted to the bar,
And farming too, and on the side
    He loves to run his car.

Frank McIntire

Occupation: President, Harper & McIntire
President South Ottumwa Savings Bank
Vice President Ottumwa Savings Bank
Vice president Hardsocg Wonder Drill Co.
Business address: wholesale 216-222 Commercial, retail 105 E. Main
Residence: 228 W. Fifth

Born in Wapello County, Frank McIntire was educated at the Iowa Agricultural College at Ames, and taught school for three terms after graduation. He became a clerk in the hardware store of Egan, Harper and Co. in 1880 and became a partner in 1881. For ten years he represented the firm as a traveling saleman. In 1891 he took his place in management and the firm was renamed Harper & McIntire. It was one of the largest wholesale and retail hardware establishments of the state.

McIntire was involved in banking and industry, and he served a term as president of the Iowa Hardware Jobbers' Association.

As a golf player he's very fair,
As a wholesaler you bet he is there;
    He helps run a bank,
    His auto he won't crank,
But any shot on the alley he will dare.

Frank D. McKee

Occupation: McKee & Potter cigar manufacturers
Business address: 119-121-123 W. Second
Residence: 215 N. Washington

"He" is a Smoker, and Most Men Are, Then "His"
Xmas Gift is at These
TWO BIG CIGAR STORES

Cigars Packed in Xmas Boxes

Any Brand in the World, and in Any Size Box
Our Humidors Keep Them Fresh
and that's important when giving cigars as gifts
Pocket Cigar Lighters
25c to $1.00

TWO BIG CIGAR STORES

PALACE   COLONIAL
Opposite Ballingall   215 East Main

Throughout the east, west, north and south,
    Do his cigars hold sway.
No place has yet been found without
    The famous Armas Del Rey.

Movers & Shakers

Charles G. Merrill

Occupation: City treasurer
Manager bond department, Phoenix Trust Co.
Business address: 114 S. Market
Wife: Mary G. Merrill
Residence: 227 E. Fifth

PHOENIX TRUST COMPANY | FARM LOANS | INSURANCE | BONDS | "WE WILL BOND YOU"
114 South Market Street

MR. MERCHANT

Do you insure the merchandise you send by parcel post? This class of insurance which costs but a trifle, not only guarantees delivery, but also covers breakage. If interested call us up.

Ins. Dept. Phoenix Trust Co.

New phone 341—233.   Old 600-B.

MARKET STREET, LOOKING NORTH, OTTUMWA, IOWA.

The block of South Market Street where the offices of Phoenix Trust were located. The Ennis Building is at right center.

This cartoon here was surely drawn
    Full many months ago;
And this, dear friends, is not a guess,
    I simply know 'tis so.

For treasurer he is no more,
    So 'twould be better far,
Instead of guarding the city's funds,
    To see him in his car.

"There are many fish in the sea
    As have ever yet been caught,"
Is the theory Merrill goes upon
    And he's right there on the dot.

But in the good old summer time
    Pickling days are hot,
So Herm then has to get to work
    When he'd much rather not.

Herman W. Merrill

Occupation: Ottumwa Pickle Co.
Business address: office, Electric Building 211 E. Second, plant 802 Hayne
Wife: Emily T. Merrill
Residence: 401 N. Green

After attending the University of Iowa for one year, Herman W. Merrill joined the family firm, J. H. Merrill & Co. wholesale grocery house, where he worked for many years. By 1914 he had turned his attention to the Ottumwa Pickle Company, where he was in partnership with P. H. Crowley, and to banking. He was a director of the Iowa National Bank and the Phoenix Trust Company, and with Charles Greenleaf Merrill owned controlling interest in the City Savings Bank. He also held banking interests in southeast Iowa and in Chicago.

He was born in Mt. Pleasant in 1858, in a log cabin which he afterwards moved to the garden of his home at 401 N. Green. The cabin, still known as the Merrill Cabin, is now located in Memorial Park.

He married Emily Temple in 1881. They had one daughter. Merrill was a member of the Country Club, Wapello Club, and Benevolent Protective Order of Elks. He was a Republican.

The log cabin in which Herman W. Merrill was born. He moved the cabin to this location, at 401 N. Green. It was later moved to Memorial Park. This photograph is thought to show Herman Merrill on the porch of the cabin.

Daniel Fowler Morey

Occupation: Secretary / treasurer and general manager
Morey Clay Products Co.
"successors to Ottumwa Brick & Construction Co."
Business address: end of Taft Ave., Fairview
Wife: Emma J. Morey
Residence: 327 W. Fourth

By 1914 Daniel F. Morey had been involved with Morey Clay Products Company, one of the largest concerns of its kind in the state, for more than twenty years. He was also known as the father of the cigar business in Ottumwa, having been a manufacturer of cigars for more than 30 years.

He was born in New York in 1851, spending the first twenty years of his life on a farm near the Catskill Mountains before coming to Ottumwa in 1871. He had learned cigar manufacturing in New York and with a partner, Ira A. Myers, maintained a reputation as the most extensive cigar and tobacco manufacturers and jobbers in the state of Iowa, operating as Morey & Myers. He later became involved in the manufacture of brick and tile, and after about 1900 he devoted his entire attention to Morey Clay Products. The company manufactured brick, tile, hollow blocks, jugs, and stoneware. He also operated a coal mine adjacent to the clay property.

He married Emma J. Graves in 1879 and the couple had four children. Morey was a Democrat, belonged to the Country Club and the Wapello Club, and was a trustee of the Ottumwa waterworks.

Morey Clay Products Co.

Successors to OTTUMWA BRICK AND CONSTRUCTION CO.

D. F. MOREY, Secretary and Treasurer

MANUFACTURERS OF

Paving Brick, Common Brick, Hollow Building Blocks, Hollow Brick, Drain Tile, Sidewalk Brick, Conduits, Stoneware, Pottery, Flower Pots, Etc.

Ottumwa Phone 288　　　Iowa Phone 1225
OTTUMWA, IOWA

There is a man in our town, who is so wondrous wise,
He always has some new idea that makes you bulge your eyes.
He says our city really needs to be made clean and bright;
The shortest cut to this result is making our own light.

John H. Morrell

Occupation: Vice president J. W. Edgerly & Co. wholesale druggists
Business address: 120-124 W. Main
Wife: Helen Morrell
Residence: 418 N. Market

For many years, John H. Morrell was one of two American directors of John Morrell & Company Ltd., along with his cousin Thomas Dove Foster. Born in England in 1864, Morrell was raised there and joined the Morrell firm in 1878, occupying positions both in England and in the United States. By 1883 he was in Chicago and in 1890 he came to Ottumwa.

He married Helen Edgerly, a daughter of Dr. J. W. Edgerly, and they had one son, George Alfred Morrell. By 1914 Morrell was no longer directly involved with the meatpacking operation but he was an officer with J. W. Edgerly & Co., his wife's family business.

In London fog, or fair Japan,
Suez or Panama,
    The natives cry
    As he goes by --
"He's the man from Ottumwa."

Claude Milburn Myers

Occupation: Confectionery, cigars, tobacco and smokers' articles, ice cream wholesale and retail
Business address: 108-110-112 E. Second
Wife: Kitt M. Myers
Residence: 440 N. Court

Claude Myers worked in his father's confectionery store in Agency until 1882 when he came to Ottumwa, working for John J. Bowles until buying the business seven years later. He continued the retail business, selling candy, but added the manufacture of ice cream on a wholesale level, as well as manufacturing candy and selling tobacco and cigars. He was an organizer and director of the Ice Cream Manufacturers of Iowa.

He married Kitt Jordon in 1912. A Democrat, he served as an Ottumwa alderman for five years and was a member of the library board in 1902 when the building was constructed. He belonged to the Country Club, the Boat Club, the Masons, the Maccabees and the Moose lodge.

Ice cream factory

Candy department and soda fountain

For many years he played the game
    Of politics and business, too.
Now all his efforts he devotes
    To making sweets for me and you.

A. Harvey Nelson

Occupation: Proprietor, Nelson Cloak Co.
Business address: 104 E. Main
Wife: Carrie Nelson
Residence: 443 W. Fifth

A. Harvey Nelson is credited with opening the first women's specialty store in Ottumwa in 1906, and he built up his business by focusing on the sale of women's outer garments. He was born in Richland in 1866 and studied at a business college in Burlington before moving to Ottumwa in 1903. He worked with a local retailer for three years before opening his own store. In just a few years, the size of his store had doubled and he employed ten people.

He also owned the Iowa Cloak & Millinery Company of Ottumwa and was vice president of the National Federation of Retail Merchants.

He married Carrie Robertson in 1891 and the couple had three daughters. A Methodist and a Republican, Nelson belonged to the Benevolent Protective Order of Elks and the Modern Woodmen of America.

Leigh Michaels

Each season he searches the nation,
To find the most fetching creation.
    He can find it, too,
      And it's always new,
His store is a style revelation.

Movers & Shakers

If you're in business, he knows how you stand,
    Whether dealing in dry goods, lumber or land.
He's always on duty, this good-natured Bill,
    And after your record he goes with a will.

William S. Otis

Occupation: Manager, R.G. Dun & Co. mercantile agency
Business address: Electric Building, 209-211 E. Second
Wife: Jessie M. Otis
Residence: 134 N. Sheridan

R. G. Dun & Co. Mercantile Agency was founded in 1841 and was the predecessor to Dun & Bradstreet. The first successful commercial reporting agency in the United States, the Mercantile Agency was a pioneer in the industry of credit reporting, an important tool in the development of American commerce.

As a local representative of R. G. Dun & Co., William S. Otis would have contributed credit reports on individuals and firms, which were added to the company's records. The 2,522 handwritten volumes are now preserved at Baker Library / Bloomberg Center at Harvard Business School.

The 100 block of Sheridan Avenue where William S. Otis and his wife Jessie lived in 1913.

Henry Phillips

Occupation: President Black Diamond Store, Ottumwa Bridge Co.,
Phillips Coal Co., Phillips Mining Co.,
President / treasurer Ottumwa Box Car Loader Co.,
Secretary Ottumwa Mill & Construction Co.
Business address: West Second "End of street car line"
Wife: Alice Phillips
Residence: 1025 W. Fourth

1890

Henry Phillips, born in Van Buren County in 1858, moved to Ottumwa in 1875 and first worked in the wholesale candy business. In 1881 he engaged in the coal business, working for his father in Phillips Fuel Co., operating mines at Phillips and Foster. In 1899 he established Ottumwa Box-Car Loader Co. with a partner,. In 1900 they constructed a factory to build loaders which would fill box cars with coal without crushing and breaking the product. He married Alice Hinsey.

Leigh Michaels

There was a time that we know
When coal was shoveled like snow.
    But now a box car
    Receives not a jar
When his "Loader" is working. Oh, no!

Maurice W. Poling

Occupation: Poling Electric Co., Iowa Auto Sales
Business address: 207 E. Second, 102-104-106 S. Green
Wife: Cassie Poling
Residence: 125 S. Willard

M.W. Poling was president of the Poling Electric Co., with interests in other electrical businesses across southeast Iowa and wide experience with electric light and power plants in various parts of the country. Born in Wapello County in 1868, he remained on the family farm until 1892 when he joined the General Electric Co. of Schenectady, New York. After a year there, he moved to Albia, Iowa, where he joined A. R. Jackson in installing the city's electric plant. He then worked for Ottumwa Railway & Light Co. for about 13 years. At the end of that time he and his brother, James F. Poling, established the firm of Poling Electric Co., installing interior and exterior lights and motors.

He was also part owner as well as manager of Iowa Auto Sales Co. of Ottumwa.

In 1906 he married Miss Katherine Cecil (the city directory lists his wife as Cassie). He was a Democrat and belonged to the Independent Order of Odd Fellows, the Royal Arcanum, and the Independent Order of Foresters. Poling's father, N. S. Poling, was a Confederate soldier who served under Stonewall Jackson in the Army of the Potomac.

Leigh Michaels

The future holds for Morris P.
    A promise grand, we know;
It won't be long 'ere we can say,
    "That dream is really so!"

When auto sales have reached their height
    And every man has two,
He figures that the airship bug
    Will just about be due.

Movers & Shakers

George Potter

Occupation: McKee & Potter cigar manufacturers
Business address: 119-121-123 W. Second
Wife: Jennie Potter
Residence: 220 Gara

George Potter began his career by selling cigars for D. F. Morey in 1884. In 1899, he entered partnership with Frank McKee in McKee & Potter. After McKee & Potter disbanded in 1917, Potter established Potter Brothers, located at 134 W. Second, continuing the cigar-making operation.

Inside the Potter Brothers location at 132 W. Second in 1924, showing cigar makers at their work stations with raw materials.

> If he ever sold a bad cigar, it has never been detected,
> With just the very best of smokes he's always been connected.
>   On holidays his only wish
>   Is just to sit and fish and fish--
> If you don't know George, your education's sadly been neglected.

James F. Powell

Occupation: President, The Courier Printing Co.
Business address: 117-119 E. Second
Wife: Mary E. Powell
Residence: 109 N. College

James F. Powell joined the Courier Printing Company company in 1889 and worked his way up to the position of publisher and editor of The Ottumwa Daily and The Ottumwa Tri-Weekly Courier. He had been associated with newspapers since starting work at The Ottumwa Democrat in 1885.

He learned the printers' trade at the Democrat and practiced it in Des Moines, Council Bluffs, Omaha, and other Iowa and Nebraska cities before returning to Ottumwa in 1889 as a typesetter on the Ottumwa Daily Courier. He later worked in the composing room of the newspaper and in the job department which produced small printing jobs for outside clients. In 1900 he moved to the business office as advertising solicitor; he was made business manager in 1901 and publisher in 1905. After the death of A. W. Lee, who was president of the Lee Newspaper Syndicate which owned the Courier at the time, Powell became vice president and treasurer of the syndicate.

He was born in 1868 in Delaware. The family moved to Illinois in 1876 and then to Ottumwa in 1883. He married Mary E. Gardner in 1907. An active athlete, Powell enjoyed shooting and rowing and "he indorses all manly outdoor sports." -- Waterman, 1914

The Courier offices in the 100 block of East Second. The current building at 213 E. Second was constructed in about 1917.

When young, this fellow named Jim,
Used to row up the river with vim,
    Now sports he eschews,
    To get the day's news.
At The Courier you'll always find him.

James Powell rowing on the
Des Moines River, about 1915.

Movers & Shakers

He has no time for sports,
 He's business all the way;
Nick runs his party in the state --
 It's the game he loves to play.

Nicholas F. Reed

Occupation: Proprietor, Central Drug Store, Opera House Drug Store
Business address: 301 E. Main, 339 E. Main
Wife: Maude B. Reed
Residence: 316 N. Court

Born in Illinois in 1868, N. F. Reed started in business as a grocery clerk and later entered the restaurant business, then took up the study of pharmacy and became a registered pharmacist by the age of 26. Though he did not attend a school of pharmacy, his study qualified him to pass the required examination to be licensed. He entered the drug business in Eldon, moving to Ottumwa in 1901 and establishing a drug store. By 1914 he was the owner of three drug stores as well as being involved in banking and manufacturing. He was the president of the Iowa Pharmaceutical Association. His deep involvement in politics as a Democrat led to a position as chairman of the Democratic state central committee. In 1914 he was appointed by President Woodrow Wilson asUnited States Marshal for the southern district of Iowa.

Promotional postcard for the Democratic State Convention of 1910.
Note the misspelling of "Ottumwa".

Look pleasant, please! For in a trice
The cap will be replaced,
And on the plate within the box
Your features will be traced.

Guy N. Reid

Occupation: Photographer, Reid Studio
Business address: 126 E. Main
Wife: Ethel S. Reid
Residence: 234 E. Pennsylvania

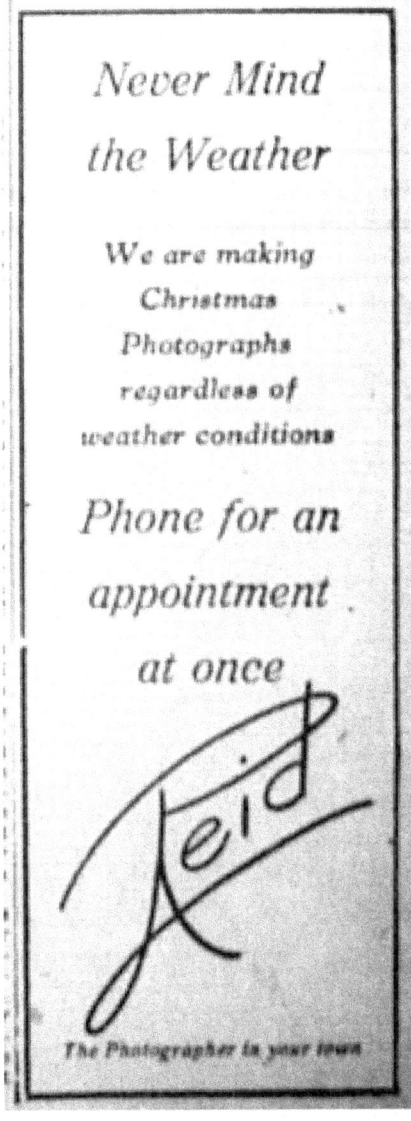

Guy N. Reid established his photo business and gallery in Ottumwa in 1905. His father, also a photographer, later joined him in the business before moving on to Illinois. Guy Reid took up the study of photography in Ohio, where he was born in 1882, and served a two-year apprenticeship.

In 1905 he married Ethel May Standish, and the couple had two children. Reid was a Presbyterian and a Royal Arch Mason, a member of the Photographic Guild of Iowa and the Photographic Association of America.

Here is the "Druggist True,"
   who always will declare
That Rexall goods are perfect --
   deny it if you dare!
All business now is he;
   but in an earlier day
Young Sargent pitched the out-curve,
   while other boys pitched the hay.

W. L. Sargent

Occupation: Druggist
Business address: 202 E. Main
Wife: Clara L. Sargent
Residence: 423 N. Market

The Rexall Store — 450 Remedies for Human Ailments. 6000 Leading Druggists in the U. S. are selling "Rexall" products with satisfaction to all

Sargent Drug, located at the intersection of Market and Main, in about 1910.

Dan Shea is happy all year round,
    No seasons dull has he,
And that is why the pleasant smile
    Upon his face you see.

When summer days, upon the wane,
    Of ice cream sales take toll,
Why then he cheerfully begins
    To sell you winter coal.

Dan R. Shea

Occupation: Confectioner, ice cream manufacturer, cigars, tobacco and coal
Business address: 333 Church
Wife: Mamie B. Shea
Residence: 120 N. Ward

DAN SHEA
333 Church Street

ICE CREAM IN SUMMER
COAL IN WINTER

Phones: Old 602, Black; New L 3090

Dan R. Shea worked in the railroad industry from the age of 15, attending school only in the winter terms. He remained with the railroad until 1899, leaving because of injuries, and then was employed by Ottumwa Steam Laundry for three years. In 1902 he became a wholesale and retail dealer in ice cream, with his store located at 333 Church, and also dealt in cigars and tobacco products. In 1910 he added coal sales to his business, creating a year-round occupation and employing seventeen men.

Born in Eddyville in 1880, he married Mamie B. Devol in 1904 and the couple had two sons. Shea was a Democrat and a Roman Catholic, and belonged to the Modern Woodmen of America, the Knights of Columbus, and the Loyal Order of Moose.

When It Gets Bitter Cold

Laugh at the weather—laugh at colds and doctor bills—by filling your bins now with Iowa's most satisfactory coal.

Smoky Hollow Coal

DAN SHEA

Sole Agent   Church Street

He's been delegate twice to the national convention,
With him it's not hard to start a contention
    On the Grand Old Party --
    It's still hale and hearty,
Although last year's count gave it very small mention.

Francis William Simmons

Occupation: President, American Mining Tool Co.
Business address: Corner Ash & Main
Wife: Elizabeth B. Simmons
Residence: 334 E. Fifth

F. W. Simmons, born in Ohio in 1854, was president of American Mining Tool, one of Ottumwa's premier businesses at a time when Iowa coal was still a considerable industry. As the child of a Methodist minister, he lived in a number of cities while growing up, attending Iowa Wesleyan University in Mt. Pleasant and the State University of Iowa in Iowa City. After graduation he taught school for several months before entering the hardware business in Ottumwa. He worked for George Haw & Co., and at the end of two years purchased an interest as a partner in Haw & Simmons in 1878. He was associated with the business for 31 years, retiring in 1906. Together with his brother George he then organized the American Mining Tool Co., which manufactured miners' tools, miners' clothing, and other supplies. Their best known products included the Little Giant drill, the Scott patent pick, and Uncle Sam overalls. The firm employed up to 75 people.

In 1890 he married Elizabeth B. Bonnifield, and the couple had three sons and a daughter. A Methodist, Simmons was a member of the Independent Order of Odd Fellows and the Masons, and was an active Republican including representing the party in national conventions.

George Budway Simmons

Occupation: Secretary / general manager American Mining Tool Co.
President Tower-Majors Candy Co.
Business address: Ash & Main; 206 S. Jefferson
Wife: Lotta Simmons
Residence: 619 E. Second

With his brother Francis, George B. Simmons organized the American Mining Tool Co., which engaged in the manufacture of miners' tools, miners' clothing, and other supplies, in about 1906. Their best known products included the Little Giant drill, the Scott patent pick, and Uncle Sam overalls. The firm, established in 1906, employed up to 75 people.

George B. Simmons was born at Fairfield in 1857. He began his career with the Belmont Carriage Works as a carriage trimmer and was later employed by the hardware firm of George Haw & Co. He was also associated with the Hardsocg Manufacturing Co. He was a director of First National Bank, First Trust and Savings Bank, and First Bank & Trust Co.

1933

He married Charlotte Rowley, and the couple had three children. He died in 1933 at age 75.

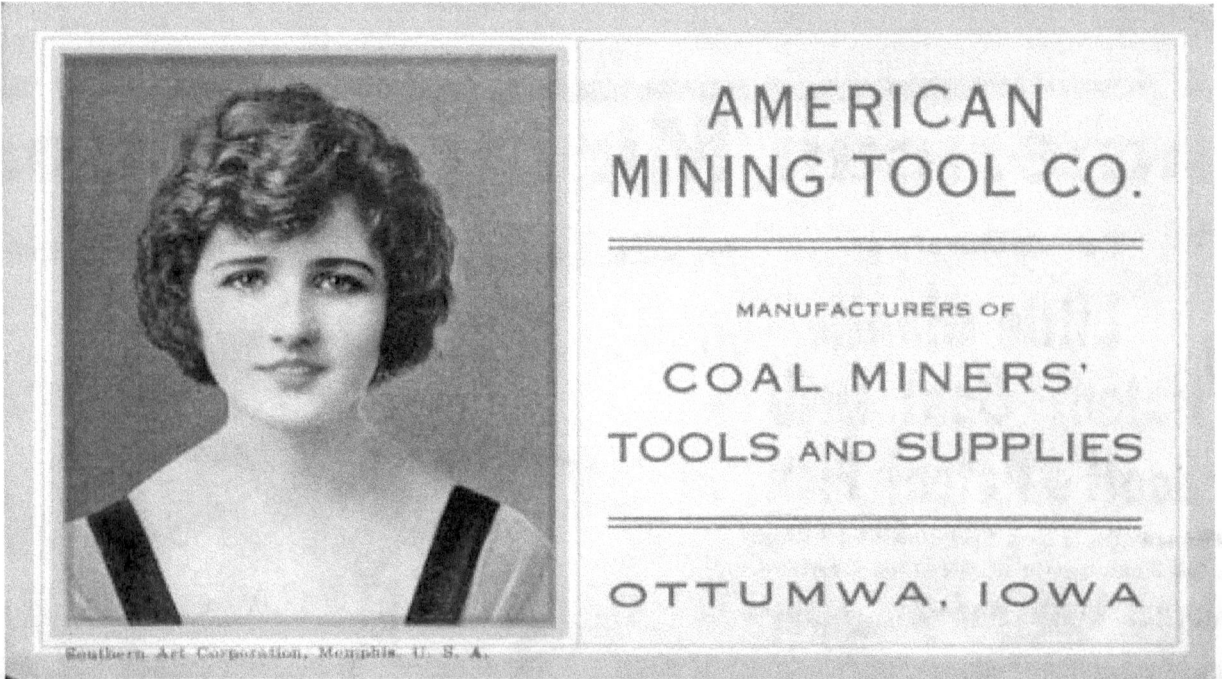

Postcard promotion for American Mining Tool from about 1915. The use of attractive models to get customer attention is not a new idea.

Leigh Michaels

This chap with intelligent mein,
Makes good tools for mining, I ween,
He has autos galore,
Will no doubt get more,
But at bowling he sure is a fien(d).

Dewey D. Smith

Occupation: Norton & Smith,
real estate, loans and insurance
Business address: 117 S. Market
Wife: Estella Smith
Residence: 233 S. Willard

Norton & Smith

Real Estate, Insurance and Land For Sale.

Frst National Bank Bldg

The offices of Norton & Smith were located in the First National Bank building, at the intersection of Market and Main Streets. By the 1920s the three-story bank had been replaced by a two-story structure which remains today but is no longer a bank.

If the land he sells to his customer,
   Is as fertile as his mind,
The man who buys a farm of him
   Most certainly has a find.

James J. Smith

Occupation: Lawyer
Business address: 22-24 Hofmann Building
Wife: Dollie H. Smith
Residence: 935 N. Court

James J. Smith was a prominent attorney in Ottumwa, starting his practice in 1879 immediately after his graduation from law school. He was also a director and stockholder of the First National Bank.

He was born in 1854 in Iowa City, and in 1885 married Mary T. Shields, a niece of General James Shields who was a hero of the Mexican and Civil Wars and a statesman who served as United States Senator from three different states. Mary Smith died in 1897, and in 1900 Smith married Dollie Healy. The second Mrs. Smith, a noted traveler, was active in the Ottumwa Hospital Association.

A Roman Catholic, Smith was instrumental in establishing General Shields Council #888 of the Knights of Columbus and was the first grand knight of the council, holding office for two years. A Democrat, he served in the state legislature and as a state senator. He was a trustee of the Ottumwa library for 12 years, of the Ottumwa Hospital Association for nearly 20 years, and of the "county insane commission" for 20 years.

After 58 years of continuous law practice in Ottumwa, Smith died in 1937 at the age of 83.

He's learned in the general law,
And very strong on torts;
From long acquaintance he's at home
In all the solemn courts.

Dr. Smith Augustus Spilman

Occupation: Physician and Surgeon
Business address: 26-28 Hofmann Building
Wife: Alice Spilman
Residence: 125 E. Maple Ave.

Dr. S. A. Spilman was born in Indiana in 1853 to a family which included three Revolutionary War soldiers, and he was educated there before coming to Ottumwa with his family in 1871. He taught school for several terms before entering what was later known as Northwestern University Medical School, where he graduated with the class of 1879. He entered into general practice and later specialized in surgery and consulting work. His education continued in New York City and in Vienna, Austria. A member of the Wapello County Medical Society, the Des Moines Valley Medical Association, the Iowa State Medical Association and the American Medical Association, he was a consultant for the Ottumwa Hospital and a local surgeon for several railroads.

In 1873 he married Mary J. Kizer, who passed away in 1876. In 1879 he married Mary Ball, who died in 1881. In 1886 he married Alice Sellers. Their son was Dr. Harold A. Spilman, who also practiced medicine in Ottumwa.

A member of the Methodist Episcopal church, he was a staunch Republican and belonged to the Masons, the Knights of Pythias, the Wapello Club and the Country Club.

1937

SPILMAN S A, wife Alice, physician and surgeon 26-28 Hofmann Bl office hours 10 to 11 a m and 2 to 4 p m, Sundays 10 to 11 both phones, r 125 E Maple av, both phones.

City directory entry from 1913-1914 stating Dr. Spilman's regular office hours -- including Sundays from 10 to 11 a.m.

This amiable Dr. S. A.
Is as young as ever today,
    When you see his warm smile,
    It would take quite a while
To guess that a knife draws his pay.

G. Frank Spry

Occupation: W. E. Jones & Co, wholesale and retail flour, feed & seeds
Business address: 307-309-311 W. Main and 101 Tisdale
Wife: Bernice Spry
Residence: 412 N. Market

Frank Spry joined the firm of W. E. Jones & Co. in 1892 and became a partner in 1902. By 1916, W. E. Jones had left the business and Frank Spry's brother John had become a partner. The business was then known as the Spry Brothers Grain Co.

A very active civic leader, Frank Spry was president of the board of the Ottumwa Hospital Association, president of the Ottumwa Chamber of Commerce, and president of the Wapello Club. He was a member of First Presbyterian Church, Rotary Club, Country Club and Elks Club. He died in 1943 at the age of 75 after a fall in his home, a duplex he had built in 1916.

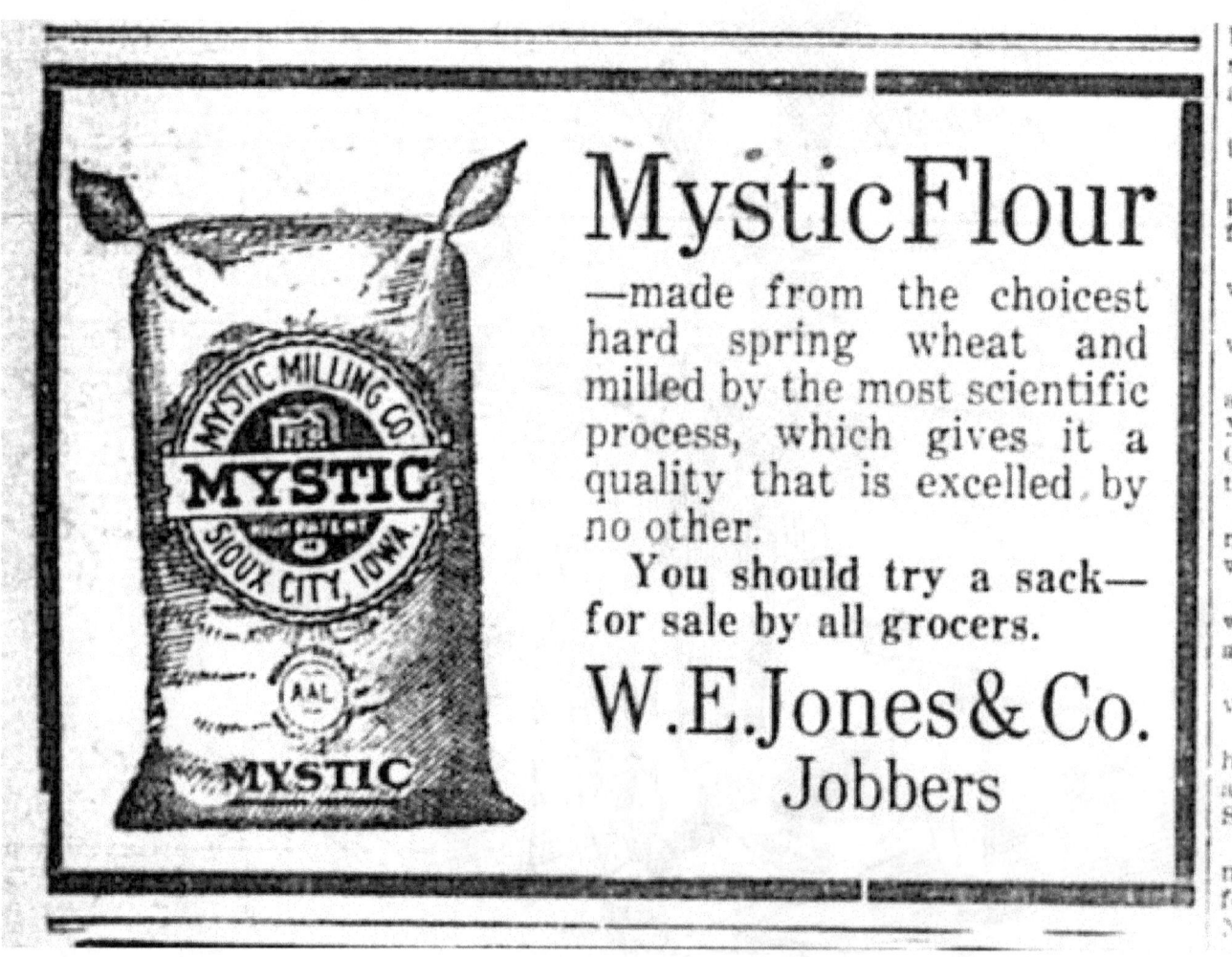

Leigh Michaels

He buys all grain delivered,
    He puts it on the cars,
And sends it into every land,
    From What Cheer up to Mars.

R. Lee Stentz

Occupation: Stentz & Bohe, cigar manufacturers
Business address: 215 E. Main
Wife: Margaret Stentz
Residence: 534 N. Green

> Men! Your Opinion, Please, on
>
> # ROBERT LEE
>
> A Nickel Cigar
> At Your Dealer's
>
> Stentz & Bohe
> Makers

Though Stentz & Bohe manufactured cigars under several labels, including Little Ben, their most-advertised brand was the Robert Lee.

This good looking fellow named Lee,
Makes the best of cigars, for 'tis he
    Who makes "Little Ben,"
    And all careful men
Choose this above others, you see.

Roy E. Stevens

Occupation: President, Stevens Shoe Store
Business address: 106 E. Main
Wife: Marie V. Stevens
Residence: 222 N. Washington

In addition to operating Stevens Shoe Store on East Main Street, Roy E. Stevens was active in Iowa politics, serving as a state senator representing Wapello County and as chairman of the state appropriations committee. In his dual roles, he balanced advocating for his constituents and their financial hardships during the Depression while noting that the state required a certain level of funding in order to provide services.

In 1935, in the depths of the national Depression, he wrote, "For example let us take the instance of a married person with no dependents, having a salary of $3,000. The computation of his tax under the present statue would be $10 on the first thousand dollars, $20 on the second thousand and $30 in the third thousand dollars of income. His exemption would then amount to $12, making a net tax to be paid of $48."

Under the proposed new tax law, "From the salary of $3,000 we would immediately deduct the $1,800 exemption provided [to a married couple], leaving a net taxable income of $1,200. The first $1,000 of this taxable income would bring a return of $10. This would leave a remainder of $200 which would be subject to the 2 percent tax or a net return of $4. Thus the tax to be derived under [the new law] against the same salary rate would be $14 as against $48."

Stevens was a director of the National Shoe Retailers' Association, and in 1936 he was named by Iowa Governor Clyde Herring to a national wildlife conference called by President Franklin D. Roosevelt.

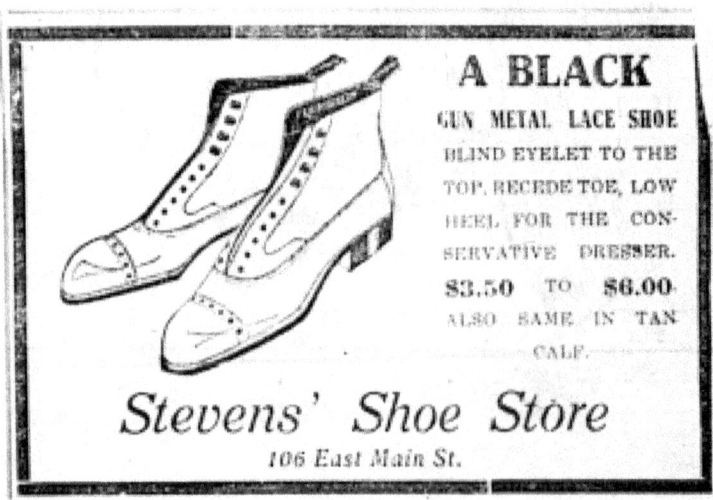

about 1935

This smiling young man they call Roy
Has shoes for your girl and your boy
    He plays with a vim
    When he's at the gym,
And volly [sic] is always his joy.

He'll go to see a ball game every day,
He likes to watch a double play.
    But if you ask him what to burn
    He will mighty quickly turn
And tell you it's oil all the way.

Theodore A. Stoessel

Occupation: Secretary & manager, Stoessel Oil Works
Business address: Corner Madison Ave. and Garfield
Wife: Anna T. Stoessel
Residence: 409 N. Madison

Theodore A. Stoessel was born in Ottumwa in 1867 and began working on the family farm at age seven. He worked for the Standard Oil Company in Iowa, Ohio, New Jersey and Pennsylvania. He served in the Spanish-American War, ending the war as a first lieutenant. Upon his return, Stoessel started a line of coal-oil wagons delivering house-to-house, later moving into refining and delivering gasoline. He was president of Stoessel Oil Works from 1909 to 1929.

He married Anna Theresa Coday in 1892 and the couple had ten children. He died in 1944 at age 76.

1944

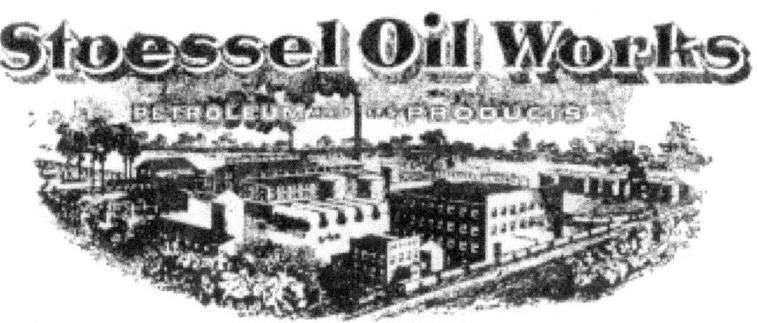

Movers & Shakers

This member of the clan
Is a fine looking man --
As a singer he has a wide reputation --
Though he works all the day
In a business like way,
At night he leads the choral delegation.

James Swirles

Occupation: dry goods, ladies ready-to-wear and notions
Business address: 112 E. Main (new phone 477)
Wife: S. Matilda Swirles
Residence: 642 N. Court (new phone 752-X)

1931

James Swirles came to Ottumwa from Pennsylvania about 1892 and worked for the S.C. Cullen Co. prior to opening his own dry-goods business in 1911, at 112 E. Main.

In 1931, after twenty years in the dry-goods business in Ottumwa, James Swirles announced his plans to close out his business and retire. According to the Ottumwa *Courier*, he had been in ill health for some time.

Ill Health Given as Reason for Local Man's Decision; Has Been Merchant Here During Past Twenty Years; New Concern to Remodel Building.

Jan 5-1931

Announcement was made today by James Swirles, local dry goods merchant, of his intention to close out his business at 112 East Main Street and retire. Announcement

Sale of Blankets AT Swirles'

A fine lot just received.

SPECIAL LOW PRICES

The largest heaviest and best looking blanket in Ottumwa for

$1.00 a pair

As good blankets as can be bought anywhere for $1.50, we can sell you at this time for—

$1.25 a pair

Our extra large, fine looking fleeced cotton blankets in grays and tans, selling for—

$1.75 a Pair

Wool nap blankets in an extra large size and weight — sold everywhere from $2.75 to $3 —at our store for

$2.25 a pair

We are getting the business, because we are giving the values.

Swirles'
112 East Main St.

Charles R. Tower

Occupation: Secretary / treasurer Tower-Majors Candy Co.
Business address: 206 S. Jefferson
Wife: Bertha B. Tower
Residence: 1137 N. Court

Charles R. Tower started his career in Kansas City, where he clerked in a shoe store for five years before returning to Ottumwa, where he was a traveling representative for J. H. Merrill & Co. for twenty years. In 1909 he resigned from the company to form his own business in association with George B. Simmons and James M. Majors, forming the Tower-Majors Candy Co. Employing an average of 65 people in the factory and six traveling salesmen, the firm manufactured high-grade chocolates for wide distribution. Tower-Majors was known as the "House of Chocolates" and the brand was known as Perfection Chocolates.

Born in 1868, Tower was the son of a well-known Civil War soldier, Lieutenant Daniel Webster "Web" Tower, who was a prisoner of war at Cahawba Prison in Alabama. When he was exchanged and sent north because of illness, he carried home with him, concealed in his wooden leg, the original copy of the song "When Sherman Marched to the Sea," which was published and distributed throughout the Union Armies.

Tower married Berta Belle Briggs in 1896 and the couple had one daughter.

"Sweets to the sweet" he offers
    In boxes gaily tied
With bright colored ribbon,
    And when you look inside
You find the best assortment
    Of chocolate bon bons, dear
To the heart of every maid
    And matron too, that's clear.

Leigh Michaels

Some men will admit that they bought 'em;
Others won't say how they got 'em;
    When Bill comes from the West,
    We all take a rest,
When he earnestly tells you: "I shot 'em."

William S. Vinson

Occupation: Walter T. Hall and Co.,
wholesale and manufacturing confectioners
Business address: 113-117 E. Third
Wife: Mae Vinson
Residence: 1108 N. Court

In 1868 at age two, William S. Vinson was brought by his parents to Wapello County, to a farm ten miles west of Ottumwa. At fourteen he became a messenger boy with the Western Union Telegraph Co. He later worked for Cockerill & Hall, wholesale manufacturers of baking powder, extracts, teas and spices, where he became a partner in 1890. The business later became Walter T. Hall & Co., wholesale confectioners. Vinson traveled for the firm as a sales representative for 17 years before and after becoming a partner. Later he managed the manufacturing end of the business.

In 1890 he married Lena Hammond, who died in 1900; they had one son. In 1910 he married Mae Martin and they had one daughter. Vinson was a Republican and a member of the Benevolent Protective Order of Elks.

Hall Candy, site of US Bank. The old Ottumwa City Hall is at far right.

HALL'S CANDIES
HAVE BEEN FAVORED BY SATISFIED PATRONS FOR YEARS

Frank Von Schrader

Occupation: President, Ottumwa Savings Bank
Business address: Main, Corner of Court (134 E. Main)
Wife: Jean Von Schrader
Residence: 223 N. Market

Frank Von Schrader followed in the footsteps of his father, who organized a private bank in Maquoketa, Iowa. Born in Chicago in 1860, Frank Von Schrader was educated in Maquoketa, where his father was initially in practice as a physician. He then attended Iowa College at Grinnell and the University of Michigan. In 1881 he began work as secretary to the general passenger agent of the Wisconsin Central Railroad in Milwaukee and was later associated with the Chicago, Burlington & Quincy Railroad. When the Ottumwa Savings Bank was organized in 1888 he became its cashier, and in 1894 was elected president.

He served three terms as city treasurer of Ottumwa. He married Jean Freeman.

If you would know the value of money, try to borrow

Many a "good fellow" needs just such a jolt to land him back on the right path. Then a savings account, however small, the beginning, if steadily added to, will lead him to financial independence. $1 starts an account.

Ottumwa Savings Bank

Oldest Savings Bank in Ottumwa
Capital, $50,000   Surplus, $111,000
Corner Main and Court

**Say to Yourslf--
"I Will Save"**

Make up your mind now that you will save at least one dollar every week. Keep in mind the thought that your account is going to grow and that some day it will be of great service to you.

Ottumwa Savings Bank

Oldest Savings Bank in Ottumwa
Capital, $50,000   Surplus, $111,000
Corner Main and Court

Leigh Michaels

On the golf links at four he'll arrive,
And to swat the small ball he will strive;
   He would give a month's pay
   If in any old way
He could increase the length of his drive.

If every man in our old town
Had the public good at heart
   As much as he;
If every man, and woman too,
Most earnestly did his part
   As well as he;
Oh, what a change there'd be.

Harrison Lyman Waterman

Occupation: Vice president, First National Bank
trustee Ottumwa Water Works; coal operator
Business address: Market & Main (131 E. Main)
Wife: Alice H. Waterman
Residence: 232 E. Fifth

Harrison L. Waterman arrived in Ottumwa in 1865 at the age of 25, having already traveled to California by way of the Isthmus of Panama in search of success in the Gold Rush. On returning to the east, crossing the Great Plains on horseback, he enrolled in Harvard University and received his Bachelor of Science degree in 1864. He served in the Civil War in 1862 and again in 1864 when he was commissioned second lieutenant in the First New York Volunteer Engineers.

On his arrival in Iowa he worked as a civil engineer with the Chicago, Burlington & Quincy Railroad, settling in Ottumwa in 1870. Apart from a few years when he lived in Kirkville and acted as superintendent of the mines of the Wapello County Coal Co., he resided in Ottumwa. Beginning in 1884 he was in charge of the coal interests of the Burlington Railroad, and was also vice president of the First National Bank. He served as mayor of Ottumwa from 1880 to 1884, and was also a state senator and a trustee of the board of waterworks. He belonged to the Masonic lodge, Grand Army of the Republic, Loyal Legion, Sons of the American Revolution, Commercial Association, Wapello Club and Country Club.

In 1879 he married Alice Hill. He had one son by a previous marriage. Alice H. Waterman was active in the Women's Christian Temperance Union and was president of the Ottumwa Hospital Association. Notably, Alice Hill Waterman is the only wife of the businessmen featured in this series who got her own individual listing in the city directory of 1913-1914.

John N. Weidenfeller

Occupation: Secretary, Ottumwa Commercial Association
Business address: Electric Building, 209-211 E. Second
Wife: Sarah E. Weidenfeller
Residence: 244 Church

John N. Weidenfeller came to Ottumwa in 1888 from Mineral Point, Wisconsin, working in the clothing business. He later operated the grain mill in South Ottumwa, and was a bank manager for Union Bank and Trust, retiring in 1948 after 23 years of service.

He was a city alderman from 1902 to 1908, later serving as a city commissioner and city parks chairman. He authorized, named and was responsible for the early development of Memorial Park. He was the secretary of the Ottumwa Commercial Club or Association from 1906 to 1917. A member of Trinity Episcopal Church, he also was secretary of the Ottumwa Country Club for 20 years.

He married Sarah Ainley. Weidenfeller died in 1952 and is buried in Ottumwa Cemetery.

COURIER, TUESDAY, DECEMBER, 16, 1913

A Round Trip to Ottumwa FREE

OTTUMWA——The Home of Quality Merchandise

WE LEAD—OTHERS FOLLOW

TRADE IN OTTUMWA---the Bargain Center of Southeastern Iowa and Northern Missouri.

Always the Best for Less at Ottumwa, Iowa

Leigh Michaels

He boosts at dawn, he boosts at noon,
    He even boosts at night.
He says we lead; that other towns
    Are lagging out of sight.
While we are playing golf or pool,
    He boosts with all his might.
It's up to us to prove that he
    Is absolutely right.

Henry C. Williams

Occupation: Blacksmith
Business address: 227 W. Main
Wife: Emma Williams
Residence: 414 N. Benton

Though Henry C. Williams was a blacksmith by profession, he seemed to have been better known in the community as an active trustee of the Ottumwa Water Works and as the father of a large family. He was born in Wapello County in 1849, but the family moved to Oregon when Henry was a small child. After the death of his father in 1855, his mother returned to Iowa and located in Ottumwa. At sixteen he began learning the blacksmith trade and by 1914 he owned a large and successful shop.

He served the community as chief of police for seven years, as deputy sheriff, and as an alderman, as well as becoming a trustee when the city purchased the water works. He was a member of the Benevolent Protective Order of Elks.

In 1873 he married Samantha Bizer, and they had three children. She died in 1882 and in 1886 he married Emma E. (Croll) Kirk; the couple had eight children.

Public Water Works, Ottumwa, Iowa.

For years he watched our river
   Flow on in its muddy way;
Its color made his flesh quiver,
   And worried him e'en in his play.
As a water trustee he got busy,
   As trustees in other lines may,
And now the result makes us dizzy,
   The water's as clear as the day.

William T. Wilson

Occupation: Clerk of the District Court, manager Griswold Abstract Co.
Business address: 107 N. Court
Wife: Edna G. Wilson
Residence: 330 Evergreen

W. T. Wilson was a native of Wapello County, born in 1864 and raised on a farm. He taught school for a while before joining the Chicago, Burlington & Quincy Railroad as a telegraph operator. He later became associated with the Griswold Abstract Company, where he remained as manager after being elected as county clerk in 1912 on the Democratic ticket.

In 1888 he married Edna Griswold, the daughter of George Griswold, an abstractor of titles. Wilson was a member of the Knights of Pythias, the Independent Order of Odd Fellows, the Modern Woodmen of America, the Woodmen of the World, and the Loyal Order of Moose.

> From Jefferson to Jackson,
> From Grover to Woodrow,
> He knows the Democrat party,
> That's how he makes it go.

Wapello County Courthouse, dedicated in 1894

William T. Wilson

Occupation: Secretary / treasurer Fowler & Wilson Coal Co.
Secretary / treasurer Alpine Coal Co.
Business address: Leighton Building
Wife: Clara Wilson
Residence: 221 E. Pennsylvania

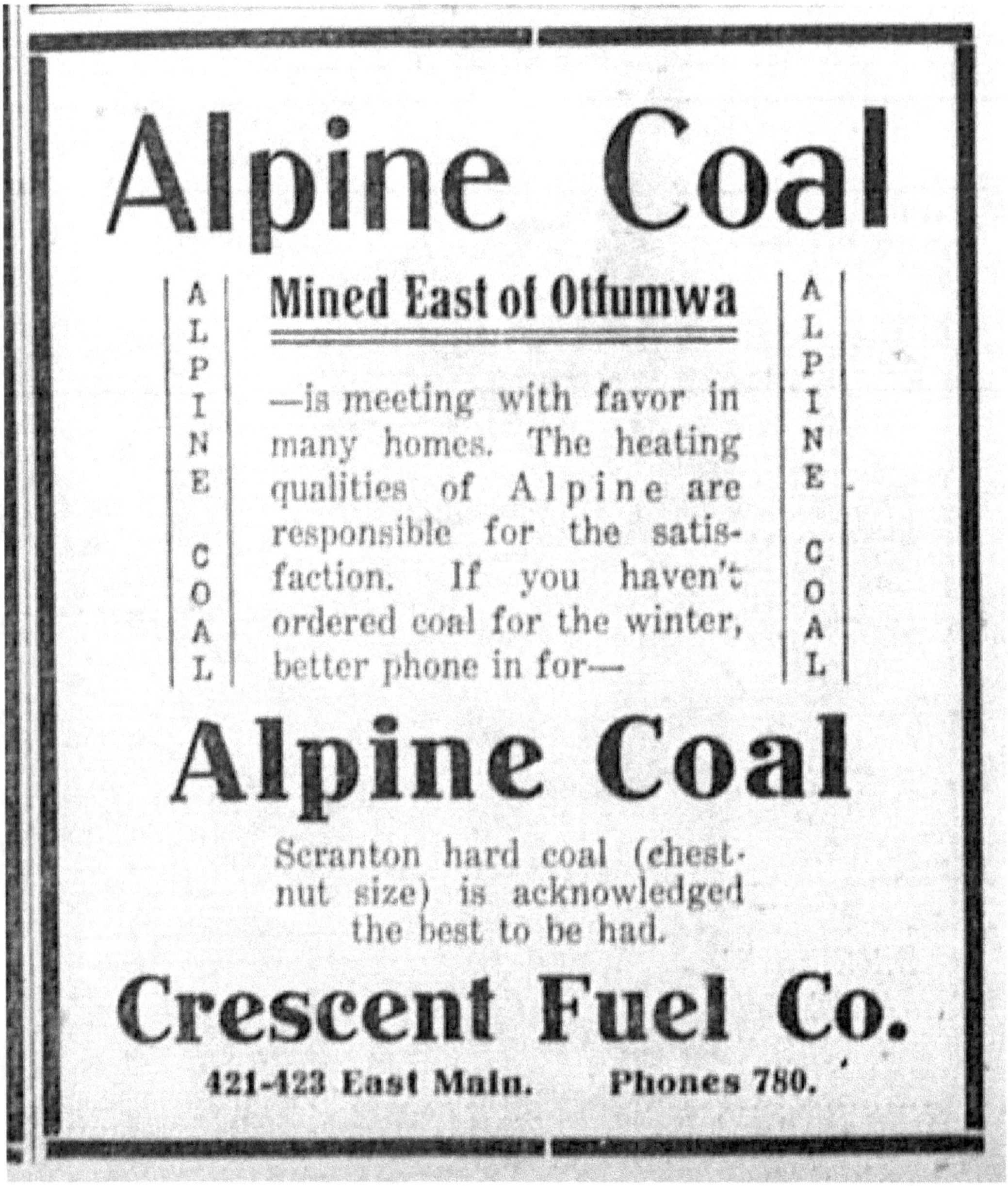

Alpine Coal

Mined East of Ottumwa

ALPINE COAL

—is meeting with favor in many homes. The heating qualities of Alpine are responsible for the satisfaction. If you haven't ordered coal for the winter, better phone in for—

ALPINE COAL

Alpine Coal

Scranton hard coal (chestnut size) is acknowledged the best to be had.

Crescent Fuel Co.

421-423 East Main.   Phones 780.

Alpine Coal, mined by the Alpine Coal Company from the Alpine mine near Cliffland, was sold by various fuel providers in the area.

Leigh Michaels

A game of golf is his delight,
    And he loves also to bowl;
But the game that he plays with all his might
    Is selling Alpine coal.

William Boyd Wycoff

Occupation: Real estate, Ennis Building
Business address: Main & Market
Wife: Sarah E. Wycoff
Residence: 412 W. Fourth

William B. Wycoff was born in Ohio (sources disagree about whether his birth year was 1835 or 1841) and came to Iowa in the 1840s, when his parents settled first in Jefferson County and in 1853 in Wapello County. As an adult he was first a farmer, then the manager of the Great Western Nursery, which achieved solid growth and profitabilty under his direction. At the start of the Civil War he attempted to enlist but was rejected because of physical disability.

His real estate business led to building numerous houses in Ottumwa as well as selling homes and farms and making loans.

He married Sarah Elizabeth Martin, whose parents came to Wapello County just a year after the area was opened for settlement. The couple had six children.

In 1904 the Wycoffs moved to Oklahoma, seeking a milder climate because of Mrs. Wycoff's health, but maintained ownership of their home on West Fourth Street and a few years later returned to live there again.

Wycoff joined the Republican party upon its founding, voting for its first-ever presidential candidate, John C. Fremont, in 1856 and later casting his ballot for every Republican presidential candidate during his lifetime -- including Abraham Lincoln.

He will sell your building
    Or buy your store;
If there aren't enough
    He knows where there are more.
If your security's good,
    He'll make you a loan;
He doesn't run short --
    He can put in his own.

George A. Zika

Occupation: Secretary / treasurer Ottumwa Supply & Construction Co.
Business address: 13-14 Anderson Building, factory Vine & Mill
Wife: Lulu Zika
Residence: 948 N. Court

Market Street Bridge, from the south bank of the river near Riverside Park. The cannon at left, a trophy from the Spanish-American War, was displayed in various locations around the city before being placed in Ottumwa Park where it remains today. The all-iron Market Street Bridge was replaced by a concrete and steel structure in 1972.

This man builds bridges of steel,
His figures roll out like a reel:
    He doesn't waste any time,
    The work fits like a rhyme,
And he's business from hat to his heel.

Who's missing?

The 91 portraits and profiles included in the Ottumwa *Courier* series and reproduced in this book covered a wide range of community leaders. But some prominent names are missing, and a number of professions and categories are not represented.

Some of the businessmen depicted here held political offices, but the mayor at the time (Patrick Leeny) and other councilmen, some of whom were just as prominent in the city, were not included. County officers such as supervisors were overlooked. There were no representatives from the community's churches or schools.

Businessmen such as candy manufacturer Walter T. Hall (head of Walter T. Hall & Co.) and Martin Hardsocg (president of Hardsocg Wonder Drill Co., Hardsocg Manufacturing Co., and Nichols Manufacturing Co.) were not included, even though other executives in those firms are featured. Joseph Dain (president of Dain Manufacturing) is missing, though it seems likely that by 1914 he was a figurehead in the business, which had merged with John Deere & Company several years earlier. Samuel Mahon, the vice president of Iowa National Bank, Iowa Savings Bank, and the Phoenix Trust Co., as well as president of J. H. Merrill and Co. and president of Morey Clay Products Co., was overlooked. J. B. Sax, one of the city's leading retailers, who died in 1930 after a half-century as a retail merchant in Ottumwa, does not appear in this list.

Other names prominent in Ottumwa's history -- Peter G. Ballingall, for example -- do not appear in this series because by 1914 they were deceased.

Perhaps the series was intended to be ongoing. If it had continued, men like Hall, Hardsocg, Dain, Mahon, and Sax might have been included. Perhaps they were invited but declined participation. Perhaps the editor's choices were made based on other considerations.

Why 91 caricatures? Why not an even hundred? The editors of the *Courier* gave no reasons -- and more than 100 years later, it seems unlikely we will ever know.

About the author

Leigh Michaels is the author of more than 100 books, including fiction, non-fiction, and local history. More than 35 million copies of her books are in print in more than 25 languages and 120 countries. She has written more than 90 romance novels, including both contemporary and historical settings, and more than 25 local history books about southeastern Iowa. She is the author of *Writing the Romance Novel*, which has been called the definitive guide to romance writing. More information is available at www.leighmichaels.com

Sources:

Baker, Chris D. *In Retrospect: An Illustrated History of Wapello County Iowa* 1992

Evans, Capt. S. B. *History of Wapello County Iowa and Representative Citizens* (Biographical Publishing Company) 1901

Illustrated Review of Ottumwa Iowa 1890 (PBL Limited) reprinted 2011

McCoy's Ottumwa City Directory 1913-1914 (McCoy Directory Company, Rockford IL) 1914

Michaels, Leigh and Doug Potter. *FIRE! Shaping Ottumwa's Landscape 1847-1999* (PBL Limited) 2017

Parrish, Sue. *Days Gone By* (PBL Limited) 2007

Lemberger, Michael W. and Wilson J. Warren. *Ottumwa* (Images of America, Arcadia Publishing) 2006

Lemberger, Michael W. and Leigh Michaels. *Ottumwa* (Postcard History Series, Arcadia Publishing) 2007

Waterman, H. L. *History of Wapello County Iowa* (S. J. Clarke Publishing Co.) 1914

Index

Note: The 91 individuals included in the caricatures are listed here only if they were also mentioned in materials other than their own profiles.

Ainley, Sarah 178
Alpine Coal Co. 52, 184
American Commercial Travelers Association 10
American Mining Tool Co. 151, 152
Amos, Ida B. 106
Armas Del Rey cigars 119
Arnold Jewelry & Music Co. 64
Atlas Acetylene Lighting Co. 79
Augustine, Adeline 101

Ball, Mary 158
Ballingall, Peter G. 190
Beamen, Alice 66
Bedwell, Brehilda 31
Bidwell, 52
Big Store 54, 55
Bizer, Samantha 180
Black Diamond Store 134
Blake, Charles F. 104
Bonnifield, Elizabeth B. 151
Bousquet, Carolina 94
Bower & Schaub Brewery 72
Bowles, John J. 128
Briggs, Berta Belle 170
Burlington Railroad 177

Carpenter, Mary C. 69
Caster, Clara E. 18
Caster, Dr. Paul 18
Cecil, Katherine 136
Central Drug Store 143
Citizens Savings Bank 8, 114,
City Savings Bank 23, 123
Claud Myers 128
Cornell Rental Agency 18
Coal Palace 104
Cockerill & Hall 173

Coday, Anna Theresa 167
Courtney, Marion 96
Cramblit & Poling 20
Cresswell & Grube 23
Crowley, P. H. 123

Dain, Joseph 190
Dain Manufacturing Co. 16, 60, 69, 190
Daggett Funeral Service 27
Daggett-Haw Transfer Co. 70
Devol, Mamie B. 149
Donelan's 34
Dungan, Myrtle A. 77
Dysart & Pearson Inc. 36

E. Daggett & Sons 27
Edgerly, Dr. J. W. 38, 66
Edgerly, Helen 126
Egan, Harper & Co. 116
Ennis Building 120

Fabritz Hardware 106
Fahrney Trust 45
Fecht, Emil 46
First Bank & Trust 152
First National Bank 31, 152, 154, 156, 177
First Trust & Savings Bank 152
Foster, George McClelland 50
Foster, Thomas Dove 126
Foster, Thomas Henry 50
Fowler & Wilson Coal Co. 52, 184
Freeman, Jean 174

Gardner, Mary E. 140
George Haw & Co. 151, 152
Gibbons Grocery 58
Gibbons Tea Store 58
Globe Tea Co. 63
Grand Opera House Co. 56
Graves, Belle 48
Graves, Emma 124
Griswold Abstract Co. 182
Griswold, Edna 182
Griswold, George 182

Hackworth Trust, 60
Hall Candy Co. 173, 190
Hall, Walter T. 190
Hammond, Lena 173
Hardsocg Manufacturing Co. 116, 152, 190
Hardsocg, Martin 190
Hardsocg Wonder Drill Co. 60, 116
Harlan, Charles F. 66
Harper & McIntire Co. 48, 64, 106, 116
Harper, W. T. 88

Haw & Simmons Co. 70, 151
Hawk Eye Coal Co. 24
Healy, Dollie 156
Hibler, Catherine (Caroline) 88
Hill, Alice 177
Hinsey, Alice 134
Hofmann, Bernard 6
Hofmann, Mrs. Bernard 6
Hofmann Building 72
Hofmann Drug 74
Hofmann, Philip Bernard 74
Hofmann, Richard Matson 74
Hoglund, Catherine 63
House of Chocolates 103, 170

Iowa Auto Sales Co. 88, 136
Iowa Cloak & Millinery Co. 130
Iowa National Bank 29, 104, 123, 190
Iowa Savings Bank 23, 63, 190
Iowa Steam Laundry 29
Iowa Telephone Co. 42

Janney Manufacturing 29
Jaques, W. H. C. 77
Jaques & Jaques 80
Jaques, Jo R. 80
J. B. Dennis Co. 31
J. F. Dings Grocery 32
J. G. Hutchison Co. 63
J. H. Merrill & Co. 123, 170, 190
J. L. Taylor & Co. 66
John Deere & Co. 15, 16, 69, 190
John H. Morrell & Co. Ltd 50
Johnson, A.W. 31
Johnston & Sharp Manufacturing Co. 82
Johnston Pressed Gear Co. 82
Johnston Ruffler Co. 60, 69, 82
Johnston, W. T. 82
Jordan, Inez 79
Jordon, Kitt 128
Julius Fecht Cigars 46
Junkins, John 18
J. W. Edgerly & Co. 38, 66, 126
J. W. Garner & Co. 56

Keefe Bros. 88
Kerns, George 109
Kirk, Emma E. (Croll) 180
Kisinger, Sue C. 60
Kitterman, Ola 41
Kizer, Mary J. 158
Kraner, Clara S. 10

LaForce, Dr. D. A. 94
Leeny, Patrick 190
Little Ben cigars 13, 162, 163
Little Giant Drill 151, 152
Lowenberg Bakery 99
Lowenberg, Chris 99
L. T. Chrisman Co. 24

SPECIAL

Buick Model 10 Roadster **$300**

This car will be advertised for sale until sold.

The price will drop $10 each day
Watch This Ad.

This car is now in the shop, being thoroughly rebuilt. Tires in fine condition — two of them brand new. New gears in rear axle.

This car is a bargain at $300. Here is your chance to get a good car cheap.

— The —
Snow Auto Co.
615 West Second St.   Ottumwa, Iowa

McCarroll Bros. 106
McCarroll, C. T. 106
McClelland, Eliza J. 50
McCullough & Lilburn 58
McElroy, Ebenezer Erskine 114
McKee & Potter 118, 139
McKee, Frank 139

Mahon, Samuel 190
Majors, James M. 170
Manning & Wellman 104
Martin, Mae 173
Martin, Sarah Elizabeth 186
Mary Jane Bread 98, 99
Matson, Isabelle (Isabella) 74
M. B. Hutchison Lumber Co. 79
Memorial Park, 123
Merrill, Charles Greenleaf 23, 123
Merrill log cabin, 123
Metropolitan Life Insurance Co. 93
Monley, Annie 58
Morey Clay Products 123, 190
Morey & Myers 124
Morey, D. F. 139
Morrell, George Alfred 126
Morrell, John H. & Co., Ltd. 50, 103, 126
Mystic Flour 85, 160

Nelson Cloak Co. 130
Norton & Smith 154

Opera House Drug Store 143
Ottumwa Artesian Well Co. 56
Ottumwa Automobile Co. 79, 101
Ottumwa Boiler Works 110
Ottumwa Box Car Loader Co. 134
Ottumwa Brewing & Ice Co. 24
Ottumwa Brick & Construction Co. 124
Ottumwa Bridge Co. 134
Ottumwa Coal Palace 104
Ottumwa Commercial Association 178
Ottumwa Courier 64, 69, 140
Ottumwa Electric & Steam Power Co. 56

Ottumwa Gas Co. 96
Ottumwa Gas, Light, Heat & Power Co. 69
Ottumwa Hospital 77, 156, 160, 177
Ottumwa Iron Works 60, 69
Ottumwa Mill & Construction Co. 24, 134
Ottumwa National Bank 31, 60, 69, 79
Ottumwa Pickle Co. 23, 123
Ottumwa Public Library 60, 128, 156
Ottumwa Railway & Light Co. 45, 136
Ottumwa Savings Bank 56, 69, 116, 174
Ottumwa Steam Laundry 29, 149
Ottumwa Supply & Construction Co. 188
Ottumwa Telephone & Electric 42
Ottumwa Waterworks 69, 124, 177, 180

Pacific Mutual Life Insurance Co. 10
Penn Mutual Life Insurance 23
Perfection Chocolates 103, 170
Phillips Coal Co. 134
Phillips Fuel Co. 134
Phillips Mining Co. 134
Phoenix Trust Co. 120, 123, 190
Poling Electric Co. 136

She Will Reemberm

such a gift as an American Beauty Electric Iron, an American Beauty or Simplex Electric Toaster, an Electric Percolator, an Electric Curling Iron, or any one of a number of beautiful electric appliances which we carry. It will be a constant reminder of you.

Poling Electric Co.

207 East Second St.   202 Either Phone

Poling, James F. 136
Poling, N.S. 136
Potter Brothers 139

Reid Studio 145
R. G. Dun & Co. 133
Robert Lee cigars 12, 162
Robertson, Carrie 130
Rock Island Railroad 109
Rosen, Clara 18
Rowley, Charlotte 152

Samuel Lilburn & Co. 31
Sargent Drug 147
Sax, J. B. 190
S. C. Cullen Co. 169
Scott, Emma F. 23

Sellers, Alice 158
Shields, Gen. James 156
Shields, Mary T. 156
Simmons, Francis 152
Simmons, George B. 103, 151, 170
Smoky Hollow Coal 149
Spilman, Dr. Harold A. 158
Sprague, Maud Leora 27
Spry Brothers Grain Co. 160
Spry, John 160
Standish, Ethel May 145
Stentz & Bohe 12, 162
Stevens Shoe Store, 164
Stoessel Oil Works 167
Sunnyslope Sanitarium 38
Swirles 169

Temple, Emily 123
Thomas Devin & Sons 58
Thompson, Eliza M. 50
Thurston, Nettie 38
Tower, Charles R. 103
Tower, Daniel Webster "Web" 170
Tower, Mabel 103
Tower-Majors Candy Co. 103, 152, 170

Union Trust & Savings Bank 79, 178
Universal cigars 46

Wallace, Melvina 58
Walter T. Hall & Co. 173
Wapello Club 56, 104
Wapello County Coal Co. 177
Wapello County Savings Bank 31, 60, 69
Waterman, Alice Hill 177
W. E. Jones & Co. 85, 160
Whipple, Catherine 85
Williams, Florence 80
W. H. Keating Insurance 87
W. J. Donelan & Co. 34
Wycoff, Lucille H. 114

Yarnell, Mary Y. 56

PBL Limited
www.pbllimited.com

www.ingramcontent.com/pod-product-compliance
Lightning Source LLC
Chambersburg PA
CBHW080246170426
43192CB00014BA/2579